ARROW BULK CARRIERS LTD.
DUNLOP HIGHWAY

INTERNATIONAL MOTORS LTD
HAMMERSMITH-1972-3-4
RELIABLE RAPID REPAIRS
INTERNATIONAL
BROOK-GREEN.
Telephones-
MOTORS LTD
HAMMERSMITH.
1972.3.4.

PICKFORDS

# CARRYING CARGO

## An illustrated history of road haulage

**Bob Tuck**

PSL
PATRICK STEPHENS LIMITED

First published in 1989

British Library Cataloguing in Publication Data

Tuck, Bob
Carrying cargo: an illustrated history
of road haulage.
1. Road freight transport to 1987
I. Title
388.3'09

ISBN 1-85260-109-4

**Cover illustrations**

**Front** The technological advances made in the bulk movement of cars are reflected in the latest phase of outfits put into operation by Cartransport Ltd. The tractor is one of 28 similar Leyland Daf 95 310 4 × 2 units which have been specifically down-plated to 28 tons to save on the excise licence duty. The triple deck Hoynor semi-trailer is built to accommodate a normal load of ten medium-sized vehicles on its air-suspended tri-axles.

**Back** Wynns seen in Wales during 1979 carrying cargo of their own particular kind. At 340 tonnes, this 45-feet diameter vessel was one of the largest of 19 similar loads that were hauled into the Texaco refinery extension being built at Pembroke.

Patrick Stephens Limited is part of the
Thorsons Publishing Group, Wellingborough,
Northamptonshire, NN8 2RQ, England.

Printed in Great Britain by Butler & Tanner Limited,
Frome, Somerset

10 9 8 7 6 5 4 3 2 1

**Front endpaper** The increasing popularity of road tankers prompted companies like Arrow Bulk to diversify from moving rubber latex in bulk, the product this company had been formed originally to move. This Atkinson 1786 was remembered as being the first vehicle to be fitted with the new powerful Gardner 150 bhp engine. It was immediately double shifted between London and Hull carrying edible oils in the Yewco tank.

**Title page** The current trend in girder trailers has also dramatically changed, perhaps not so much in shape but certainly in both size and capacity. This GEC photograph shows TM 1120 pausing for breath *en route* from Manchester to Rugby in 1973. PGO 711E, the leading Scammell Contractor, had chassis number 21210 and was in the second batch of 240 ton tractors when delivered to Pickfords in June 1967.

**Inset** Carrying one motor vehicle on top of another one never seemed a logical idea, although an emergency situation was always to be the exception. This Ford Motor Co photograph illustrates a specially-angled, custom-built recovery vehicle on a Motor T chassis loading up a similarly chassised motor car.

**Rear endpaper** What was to change dramatically the operation of goods vehicles was the concept of containerization. Instead of having slowly to remove the load piece by piece, one crane movement saw the container and the load moved in its entirety. Stevens of Great Ayton were specialists in long steel work, so their skeleton type of trailers were easily adopted for early use in this type of traffic. Driver of the Scammell Handyman KVN 714E is Bill Cowens, the semi-trailer being of Walker manufacture, although at that time it had not received the now virtually mandatory fitment of container twist locks.

# Contents

# Preface

No matter whether you call it haulage or distribution, carrying cargo by road is the lifeline of our country. Situated off the mainland of Europe we depend entirely on the links between our ports and our factories, our railheads and our airports, and virtually every other place in between. The hauliers of millions of tons of cargo each year are rarely appreciated but never forgotten.

Their tool of the trade used to be called the lorry but now seems to have evolved into the truck. *Carrying Cargo* examines the evolution of these load carriers although I accept there is no book large enough to show the flair and imagination regularly demonstrated when men and machines co-ordinate to carry virtually anything imaginable.

# Acknowledgements

In researching a book touching on such a wide variety of topics as *Carrying Cargo*, I have needed the help, support and guidance of many people. It is to them that thanks must be extended.

Many have given help in finding photographs that hopefully have never been used in book form before. Those that should particularly be mentioned are Roger Annis, Vic Cole, Dennis Harris, Ken Glendenning, Richard Joyce, Tony Kimber, Tony Knowles, Peter Lee, Tom Llewellyn, Fred Robinson and Tim Wayne.

Others have spent hours searching records for details so that my captions may have a little meaning. I only hope I have done them justice: George Baker, Alan Martin, John Mollett, Howard Nunnick, John Wynn.

Thanks, too, to those who have taken the time to explain the finer points of transport and offer some stories of life to boot: to Alan Cooper, Bobby Durham, Roger Elsom, Doug Golding, Alastair Carter, George Neville, Ronnie Nimmo, Frank Strange and especially Eddy Tomlinson.

In never forgetting my wife Sylvia, I would also like to mention John Thompson, a man who gave me time and guidance in my formative years. The happy days we had together will never be forgotten.

# 1. To be rigid or to articulate

In less than a century, road transportation has been the scene of some dramatic change. The horse and cart vehicle predominating in the 1800s may still be seen at work in some northern towns, but generally the evolution of the lorry has produced a highly efficient unit expected to move anything required.

The progress has not been without some acute heart searching. Those early manufacturers around at the birth of the internal combustion engine were in a difficult position in knowing which way to tackle the demands made for goods-carrying vehicles. The options available to them followed three distinct courses. The basic saloon car was quickly shorn of its rear passenger compartment to be converted into a load-carrying vehicle, and many an adapted Ford Model T was the original vehicle for some of the big names in modern day transportation.

The established steam traction-engine builders like Foden were producing smaller fire-propelled machines that were strong, capable and could be very quick. But the exciting way forward was to go with the new breed of manufacturers sprouting up to produce the purpose-built vehicle, firstly with petrol and — ever since the experimentation of Nottingham bus operators Bartons — with the diesel oil engine. But one conflict that has not been decided one way or the other for almost 70 years is whether hauliers should opt for a rigid lorry or an articulated one. The potential for either can on occasion overlap, making the eventual decision just a case of personal preference.

One of the main selling points of the articulated outfit today is the potential of interchanging trailers to maximise use of the expensive tractor unit. But when Scammell Lorries initially introduced their motor show success of 1922, they were at pains to emphasize that their new vehicle, which to you and me was simply the articulated outfit at its birth, was not in fact hauling a trailer, but was simply a rigid vehicle which happened to bend in the middle.

Trailer-hauling vehicles suffered from an excessive premium in operating costs, but the bending rigid poked its head through this loophole and claimed an identity all of its own. Once legally accepted, Scammell, Carrimore Six Wheelers, Taskers and others were to produce sophisticated, semi-automatic couplings for their semi-trailers, keenly snapped up by many, including, rather strangely, the railway operators, who found the Scammell Scarab type artic a boon for their operations. This early double fork and roller mechanism with built-in landing wheels was rather limited in its capacity, so uncoupling the heavier artics was still a workshop job that normally utilized a massive oil drum as a support once the tractive unit was driven away. The fifth wheel coupling we know of today was still waiting to be invented.

The rigid fraternity on the other hand were offered a varied range of stronger four-wheelers in the guise of vehicles like the Leyland Beaver and the AEC Mammoth, but in 1930 came the birth of the epitomy of British lorries, the rigid eight-wheeler. The concept was initially permitted to allow the heavy steamer vehicle a way back from its dwindling market share, and naturally Sentinel, with their famous DG8 multi-wheelers, were first on the scene. However, once the likes of Armstrong-Saurer, Albion, ERF and many others had got their designs sorted out, the steamer's days, in general haulage circles at least, were numbered. Even Foden, who seemed to mourn the passing of steam, were to produce their DG 6/15 in 1937 and were to champion the cause of rigid eights for nearly 30 years.

Many haulage contractors, however, had little chance to become involved with this new concept of vehicles, because most smaller operations had to depend on second-hand vehicles. They had to adopt a strange rule of thumb to get phenomenal work out of some of the lightweights, as overloading seemed a way of life. The normal procedure was to buy a

$2\frac{1}{2}$ tonner in whatever condition could be afforded, then double its capacity overnight by just calling it a 5 tonner. Then it was loaded with $7\frac{1}{2}$ tons of payload, but driven considerately so that its back was not broken.

With the arrival of the Second World War, the rigid-artic contest was put on hold as efforts were put into a more important battle. However, one noteworthy effect of these war years was to allow rigid eights to haul drawbar trailers, offering not only a larger capacity vehicle with an increase in the permitted overall length, but also eight more potential tons towards a greater legal payload margin. To many this proved to be the trump card, because the rigid and the wagon and drag as they were known were to reign supreme, although one drawback was that such an outfit had the statutory requirement of having to carry an attendant, or trailer mate as he was known. The mate's main task was to assist in the manoeuvring of this lengthy combination, especially in hitching and unhitching the drawbar trailer, or 'dangler' as it was affectionately christened. Reversing the drawbar was an art in itself, only appreciated by those who have lost buckets of sweat in trying to master this difficult technique!

Getting over the hostilities must have been difficult enough, but the nationalization of transport operations in 1948 was to turn the vast majority of haulage on its head. The concept that formed British Road Services was obviously brilliant in its ideal to build an efficient network of transport operations, what it did stifle was the natural flair and imagination which is prompted by downright competition.

Initially BRS took over the hauliers' own vehicles, best described as weathered with the rigours of war. Their replacements were brand new, the heavyweights being of diverse makes including Foden and Leyland, although retired driver Ronnie Nimmo recalls being given the new BDC 66, one of the last Maudslay Meritor eight-wheelers to be built. Having the AEC 9.6 litre engine it was far quicker over the ground than the ponderous Gardner-powered Fodens. It was always able to surmount hills in at least one gear higher but when going down hill, Ronnie recalled, the vehicle regularly gave him nightmares.

Air brakes had been made available on some goods vehicles as early as 1934, but most manufacturers, Maudslay included, persisted in specifying a hydraulically-operated system with vacuum assistance, the type which predominates in our modern-day saloon cars. This type of braking did not instil a great deal of confidence in drivers, especially with 22 tons and more all-up weight, so many sensible chauffeurs adopted a little saying — you go down a hill in the gear that you would use to come up it. For the lowly Gardner 6LW engine-powered vehicles that normally meant bottom gear.

In theory the Maudslay's brakes should not have been any worse than others which were only fitted as standard to six out of the eight wheels, but Ronnie found his particular vehicle very prone to total braking loss. He always carried a bottle of brake fluid with him to replenish the reservoir mounted on the rear bulkhead just behind the driver's seat. He recalls many occasions of massive back pressure in the system spurting the brake fluid out of the pin hole breather in the reservoir cap, and splattering it on to the inside of the cab roof above him.

Whilst tramping the countryside, Ronnie grew to accept the slight idiosyncrasies of the Maudslay's brakes, but once the vehicle was taken off him and put on the demanding overnight trunk route to London, the cockney shunters simply refused to work it as it continued to frighten the living daylights out of them. The subsequent conversion fitment to air brakes might have been expensive but it made the Meritor into a far better machine.

Lorry driving even 30 years ago required a special breed of men. They were made to be oblivious to the deafening noise coming from that massive engine hump which demanded most of the space in the interior of the cab. In the height of summer the heat generated made this working compartment into a sweat box, whilst lacking in any form of heater, which meant the traditional winter garb of every lorry driver was his ex-army greatcoat, hat and muffler. You could not even leave your wagon on a night without deciding first if it was going to freeze or not. If the temperature was dropping then the water was drained from the radiator, and you had to catch what you could in a couple of containers. You put the caught water back in the next morning and hoped you had enough to limp along to the nearest tap before you boiled dry. Antifreeze was a luxury that most vehicles went without.

Back amongst truck building developments, the 1950s saw the arrival of the modern-day fifth wheel coupling. Scammell offered a beefed-up version of their Scarab-type mechanism but this met with little favour and it was up to people like Davies to produce the universally more acceptable hitch that was to push the artic ahead in the operational stakes, with the opportunity to make multiple use of less expensive interchangeable semi-trailers.

On paper the artic may have had the edge in having the potential to provide more earning revenue, but on the road many a driver was to feel more at ease with a rigid multi-wheeler. True, they could be a handful in town driving and negotiating some of these mini roundabouts made you work hard at the steering wheel, but at least a rigid wouldn't jack knife. It was every artic driver's nightmare to feel that drive axle lock up and the pushing effort from the trailer simply turn the tractor round on its hitch, with the side of the trailer crunching into the cab and the destiny of whatever load was being carried in the lap of the gods.

Artic drivers were also regularly blasphemed at as their efforts up only the slightest of inclines with inferior surfaces were normally greeted with the most dismal of failures. The slip-sliding efforts of a lightly-laden drive axle were no match for the unstoppable rigid, with a friendly wave from the overtaking multi-wheeler being of little consolation to the frustrated artic driver as he waited for the over-worked gritting wagon to appear.

The eight-wheelers now running at 24 tons gross had a pleasant, balanced look similar to the maximum weight four-wheelers now allowed to gross up to 14 tons. Bridging the gap at 18–20 tons were the six-wheelers which always seemed to look more ungainly. Having two axles at the rear on twin tyres made vehicles like the Leyland Hippo look all back end, but they did not look as odd as the AEC Mammoth Minor which only had single tyres on its third rearmost axle. This tag axle-type appearance was a strange sight, but was to gain far better acceptance in the 1980s, especially with Scania marque vehicles as they adopted this concept with some of their 38 ton capacity artics.

The Mammoth Minors may have been a rarity but seen in slightly more numbers was the six-wheeler, having two steering axles at the front and one drive axle at the rear. It was commented that only the Chinese would build a six-wheeler with such a 'wrong way round' design, so since that time 'Chinese Six' is a nickname that has stayed with that fine-looking truck.

The late 1950s and early 1960s were times of both consolidation and development in road transport. In February 1961, Transport Equipment (Thornycroft) Ltd were acquired by AEC although the big T was to be seen for many more years than the long-gone Maudslay motif. Scammell and Albion had also been bought out, but their identity remained intact as they became a strengthening force to the Leyland empire. Also in 1961, Guy Motors suffered from financial problems and in October of that year they were bought by the car makers of Jaguar.

The first stretch of motorway in the guise of the Preston bypass was soon joined by the southern part of the M1 and M10 link, which was opened by Ernest Marples in November 1959. The effect on vehicle construction was dramatic, as overnight, from 1 May 1957, long-distance vehicles which had been shackled at speed limits of 30 mph (over 3 tons) and 40 mph (under 3 tons), could now travel on these stretches of road at whatever speed they liked.

Foden were one of the first to show legally what drivers of their vehicles had known for years, that the performance of their two-stroke engines could be quite breath-taking. In early 1961 an experimental eight-wheeler running at 24 tons gross recorded an average speed of 60.5 mph over 130 miles of motorway with a fuel consumption of 8.9 mpg. The engine used was the Foden 4.09 litre Mark IV supercharged two-stroke producing 210 bhp at 2,200 rpm. Driving through 5.2:1 rear axle ratios gave a geared top speed of 64 mph, making the lively average very respectable.

The fibreglass S21 cabbed eight-wheeler was also an exercise in weight saving as fuelled up it tipped the scales at less than 7 tons, so allowing a clear 17 tons of payload. Fellow Sandbachians ERF were also experimenting with a 17 ton payload-carrying eight-wheeler, this one being powered by a Rolls-Royce B81 6.5 litre petrol engine producing 195 bhp at 3,750 rpm. Top speed was 63 mph, whilst fuel consumption was not totally excessive at 4–5 mpg.

Leyland too were to produce their high-performance Power Plus range getting over 200 bhp from their 680 engines whilst the faithful Gardner followers were rewarded with the 150 bhp 6LX engine, what many people feel was to be the Patricroft manufacturers' finest production; not exactly a greyhound, but a big improvement on the 6LW, with typical Gardner reliability still assured.

Even with the dramatic changes in engines and performance, for over 40 years the choice between rigid and artic had been a close run thing, but in 1965 the legislators dealt a body-blow to the eight-legging rigid when they allowed all newly-built artics of suitable structure to run at 32 tons gross all-up weight. It is true that rigid eights were given a theoretical increase to 28 tons gross, but this was only permitted if the outermost axles were at least 26 ft apart.

The 4 ton margin was not easily won for the artics because those on four axles had to have an outer axle spread of at least 38 ft whilst not exceeding a total overall length of 42 ft 7¾ in. This was rather complicated, although S. Harrison & Sons of Sheffield strangely contended that the bonneted Scammell Highwayman with set forward front axle was one of the few four-axled artics that could legally run at the higher 32 ton weight band. It was far easier to conform to the letter of the law by either running at 30 tons on four axles or using five axles for the extra 2 tons weight, as that restrictive wheelbase requirement was not as harsh for the more axled type of vehicle.

Truck manufacturers were caught a little bit cold by the demand for tractive units, although Scammell found quite a following for their lightweight six-wheeled Trunker II. Foden also came up with something special and although being quite a head-turner, its concept may have been too extreme for it to obtain a big following.

The Twin Load was in essence based on a standard S.34 cabbed rigid eight-wheeler. However, at the extreme rear of the vehicle, part of the normal platform was removed and in its place was put a fifth wheel coupling plate. To this was hitched a short, single-axle semi-trailer so the outfit was in fact a five-axled artic with two distinctly separate loading areas. At less than 10 tons in unladen weight, this Foden offered a clear 22 tons in payload potential, but even though it gave far better traction with its double drive bogie than any normal artic was capable of and it was virtually impossible to jack knife, the Twin Load never sustained its initial impact.

Even though both vehicles and road structure were improving, enhancing transport's efficiency was not solely a matter of how quickly a driver could get from A to B, but more a case of how quickly a driver could load up at A or unload at B. Specialist trucks apart, the vast majority of vehicles around at this time had platform bodies. The flat, as it was known, could be loaded from the side by fork-lift truck, from overhead by crane or from both sides and rear in the traditional manner known as hand-balling. Once the vehicle was fully loaded, the driver had to ensure firstly that his cargo would not shift, and secondly that it was protected from the elements during the course of its journey. Loads of steel were detested by some as being cumbersome and awkward, but at least they could be quickly chained down and warwicked tightly into position. Virtually every other cargo had to be painstakingly sheeted by tarpaulin and tightly roped in a very correct manner.

Roping and sheeting was and still is very much an art, with the completed outfit being an obvious reflection on the driver's ability. Unfortunately he had little time to admire his handiwork for all to soon he would have to unsheet and unload prior to a repeat performance when the next load was picked up. This procedure was time-consuming enough but at least it was down to the driver and how quick he could work. Waiting in a queue simply for his turn to load or unload was the most frustrating of daily events, and perhaps the docks were the worst of all where varying working practices meant that literally days could just be lost as a driver waited in line for his turn. It was for this reason that National Productivity Year coined the slogan 'Turn that lorry round', but in places like the docks the plea simply fell on deaf ears.

What was to change transport operations so much was firstly the concept of containerization, and secondly the invention of Gerald Broadbent known as the curtainsider Tautliner. The principle of containers is seen so much in use today that it is virtually taken for granted. True, time still has to be spent initially loading up a container and finally removing the cargo at its point of delivery, but these two points could literally be on opposite sides of the world. The big boon with the container was that all the handling in between these points was done in one single lift.

Special ocean-going ships were built to accommodate this new breed of traffic which was standardized on fixed container lengths of 20 ft and 40 ft, both being of equal width. Goods vehicles, too, were specially adapted to secure these containers by means of a system of twistlocks mounted on the corners of the carrying vehicles. The twistlock was a simple mechanism operated by turning a toggle bar through 90°. This turning movement engaged a key-type lever into the bottom of the container and thus secured it tightly to the carrying vehicle in a quick and efficient manner. Releasing the container was just a reverse movement of the twistlock, freeing it for unloading purposes in a matter of seconds.

Some rigid vehicles were fitted with twistlocks into their platform bodies, but it was to be the versatile artic combination that was the biggest favourite for this type of traffic.

It was in 1969 that Gerald Broadbent of Boalloy came up with the idea of the Tautliner, the first one being of a modest 20 ft length on a single axle semi-trailer. Its construction is perhaps to have a van body in-built, but making the sides of a tarpaulin type material which could be pulled aside on a system of runners like curtains, revolutionized cargo handling.

The continental-type tilt trailer had been around for some time but it had sideboards and a substantial framework underneath its tarpaulin shroud, and getting access, especially into the side of a tilt, was a particularly long process. The tilt could remove its roof for overhead crane loading, so in that respect it had an advantage over the curtainsider.

Securing the Tautliner was achieved by a system of buckles and tensioners running down the side of the canvas sides, so to many drivers the advent of containers and Tautliners meant they would never sheet another load again.

Whilst the rear part of the lorry was undergoing a period of radical thought, the front end or cab was also under transition. The coach-built versions were certainly a fine construction with their varnished ash frame woodwork looking extremely impressive, although Fred Robinson was one man who looked at the cab through a more costing eye. His company of F & F Robinson, based at Stockton but having long-standing connections with the south of England, was well-known for its overnight trunk between Teesside and London. Following rare dispensation granted by the local police, the drivers from Stockton changed vehicles with their colleagues from Ware, on the High Street at Newark. Swapping round in this way meant all the respective drivers reached home at the end of the shift as it was only the vehicles and not their drivers that reached the other end of the country.

The nightly trunk ran on an exacting timetable but the driver was still the only person in the vehicle, making the nearside of the compartment rather superfluous. Fred also noticed that when a cab came in for repair after an accident it always seemed to be nearside damage, as naturally if a driver had the choice he would always swerve away so he was furthest from the impact point. Looking through Fred's eyes, it was natural to query the payment of £700 for a full cab when only a half cab would cost £220.

Up to the late 1950s Fodens had produced some single-deck touring coaches which, following the vogue of Leyland and others, saw the driver cocooned in his sleek half cab. Fred felt this type of cab would look fine on an articulated tractor unit, but just before the order was put in Foden decided to phase out their coach production.

Determined to put his plans into action, Fred worked very closely with Ted Lowe, head of the Foden welding shop to produce something similar. The finished product saw immediate adoption on to the Foden dumper although Fred bought 14 of these half-cab tractors, putting them out on to the overnight trunk to London. With the provision of a window in front of the driver's knees the half cab did give excellent all round vision, especially when shunting round London, and as far as the boss was concerned it did prevent the carriage of unauthorized passengers. The limited cab heater, now with only half the space to heat, could easily dispel the winter chills although driver Roger Elson found the half cab did have one or two rather obvious drawbacks.

It was some years later when Roger was given new NFL 766F, a sister machine to NFL 765F. The 180 Gardner-powered artic tippers run by St Ives Sand and Gravel out of Huntingdon were double shifted for the first four years of their life on a demanding triangular route encompassing Kent, the Potteries and Leicestershire. It was not until the night shift was dropped and the vehicle stood during winter nights that Roger realized what extra precautions he had to take. With having no form of interior trim the bare steel roof naturally attracted condensation which froze during the cold night. Fired into life at 6 o'clock for the first delivery of sand, Roger recalled it was like jumping into a shower as the water droplets thawed out and gravity did the rest.

Even having a relaxing snooze in the half cab was a work of art. The feet had to be perched on the heater box, your bottom resting on the edge of the seat and your head forced up in the corner with the side window. Not really a suitable resting position, but lorry drivers were men who were specially trained to be able to sleep on a clothes line when they were tired enough.

One big bonus of the half cab is that they did allow for better access into the engine compartment than the traditional fixed cab but when cabs were made to completely tilt forward, this attraction was obviously ruled out. The gaunt lines of the half cab did little to enhance the reputation of the image-conscious haulier, so even cost counting operators like Robinsons phased them out from general haulage operations.

With the influx of continental vehicles in the late 1960s, cabs also grew in size as the custom-built sleeper cab gradually demanded acceptance. Many a wagon driver had for many reasons been forced to spend many a night in his cab and what a torturous experience that could be. The sleepers with single or even double bunks were comfortable, accessible and obviously could be more hygienic when compared to some questionable 'digs' of the past.

The artic tractor unit was a natural for fitment of the sleeper cab, having ample space to accommodate it in the physical gap ahead of the semi-trailer headboard. In fact sleeper cab tractor units became so much a part of the norm that the legislation was eased in 1983 to raise the overall length limit of artics to 15.5 m. This extra half metre was purely to allow for better coupling freedom to the standard 12.2 m or 40 ft trailer with the longer sleeper cab units.

The rigid could only seeth at the increasing popularity of the artic. True, some of them were fitted with sleepers but such fitment meant a natural reduction in the length of the payload carrying body behind the cab. The gross weight difference was narrowed in June 1972 when eight-wheelers were allowed to run up to 30 tons, but this narrow gulf changed to a dramatic void on 1st May 1983 when artics with five axles or more could run up to 38 tonnes. The rigid vehicle seemed destined for oblivion were it not for a number of minor happenings coinciding virtually together.

The main popularity surrounding artics was the interchangeability of the load-carrying semi-trailers which could be hitched or unhitched within seconds. The rigid could not be made to split in half, but with the resurgence in interest of demountable bodies, the popular articulated concept did not look so unreachable.

The use of demountable bodies is long-established, and hauliers of the 1920s demonstrated their versatility with interchanging platforms, van bodies, tipping frames and even passenger carrying charabanc bodies for use on weekend trips to the seaside. These early concepts may have relied on a block and tackle pulley system suspended from the garage roof to lift the bodies clear, but the 1980s version now has the use of many technological advances to aid the interchange.

Today's systems bring into use either air suspension on the drawing vehicle, which when exhausted drops the rigid down and leaves the body suspended up on its fixed landing legs; or hydraulic systems in the supporting legs of the body which when activated simply lift the body and its load clear of the road-going vehicle, allowing space for it to be driven away with the body left where desired.

One thing always against the wagon and drag was that it had always been a handful to manoeuvre and although the need to carry a costly driver's mate was phased out, they were still difficult to reverse. Many potential operators fought shy of the big combinations in favour of the artics, but with a minor change in trailer design this problem was totally surmounted. The conventional drawbar trailer has always had one axle at the front, normally linked to the drawbar, and the second and other axles located at the rear. However, once the two or even three axles were located centrally and the drawbar simply attached to the trailer frame, reversing the entire outfit was now just as simple as an oversize artic.

The next practical application to affect the wagon and drag was its speed limitations, for it had always lagged at least 10 mph behind the limits of the basic rigid or conventional artic. But in 1981 the variation of speed limits order brought together the speed limits of all comparable goods vehicles when it allowed rigids, artics and wagon and trailer combinations to run up to 60 mph on motorways and 50 mph on dual carriageways.

The gap between the rigid and the artic was gradually being reduced. If it needed a final touch then the fitment of sleeper cabs above rather than behind the normal driving compartment swung many operators who did not really have the need or desire to run at the higher weight bands allowed for the multi-axle artics. It proved to be just as well for the rigid to regain this ground because it was seeing its long-time leadership amongst one section of lorries gradually being overtaken.

**Above** Long before legislation restricted the weight of general haulage vehicles, *Lord Roberts* is seen hauling 34 tons of bricks in its 62 ton all-up weight. The Foden eight horsepower road locomotive no 457 was fitted with a three-speed gearbox, that was new in 1900. The drive axle was fitted with Boulton-patented, wood-block-sprung wheels, primarily intended to cause less damage to the road surface, and also to absorb the shocks from the rough stone sets.

**Below and bottom** It seemed a natural progression to retain the drawing vehicle with drawbar trailer, and although the Foden steamer has an obviously dated look about it, the Ford car-based unit hauling a Carrimore trailer belies its era of about 1937. VM 3059 was a Class C Foden tractor No 12896, new to Parker's of Ancoats, Manchester in July 1928. Its main work was hauling cut lengths of imported timber from Manchester docks to the Ancoat's yard. The odd item on top of the Foden chimney is an additional spark arrester made from wire.

In contrast to the simple drawbar pin, the automatic coupling of the new articulated vehicles seemed complicated in the extreme. The in-built landing legs did, however, mean that the semi-trailers could be deposited anywhere that was reasonable. The articulated concept dramatically increased the potential of the mechanical horse, these Karrier Cobs being direct competitors to the similar three-wheeled Scammell. BWT 663, destined for Harrogate Corporation, was new in 1936, although the Cobs were first produced in 1931, with these two being built at the Karrier factory in Luton.

The concept of the eight-wheeled rigid goods vehicle was first produced in a Sentinel steamer application in 1930. It was four years before the arrival of the first non-steamer eight-legger, when hauliers could really take advantage of the big payload potential offered in the 22 ton gross weight limit of a vehicle which just oozed with strength and reliability. Albion Motors began eight-wheeler production in about 1935, their rigid GKA 56 dating from 1940. It is seen about to leave Distington Engineering in about 1957. Johnston Bros themselves had reformed after nationalization, their pre-1950 fleet of eight vehicles and two trailers being taken over in November 1949 to form the RHE unit No C215, part of the Carlisle Group.

Bridging the gap between four and eight wheelers, the six wheeler never seemed to have the same balance in its appearance, its traditional double drive bogie seeming to make it rear end heavy. Rankin's Atkinson BBR 258 dates from 1950, it being based at the newly-opened Fleet Street depot at North Ormesby on Teesside.

Perhaps of even stranger appearance were the rare AEC Mammoth Minor lightweight six-wheelers. As well as having only one of their two rear axles driven, the trailing axle was only equipped with single as opposed to twin tyres. Currie's were one of the biggest hauliers on Tyneside prior to nationalization. The AEC is seen about 1938 *en route* to Fuller Electrics at Walthamstow.

First called the 'four in hand', after the horse and cart system of having four horses controlled by one driver, the six-wheeler with two front steering axles has forever since been christened the Chinese Six. Although technically always 2 tons below the limit allowed for the double drive six-wheeler, this fine-looking vehicle always tended to run at the same 18–20 ton weight limit. MEH 372 dates from 1948, it being part of the BRS Carlisle Group controlled from 83, Lowther Street, Carlisle, although this Leyland Steer was probably based at the Whitehaven depot. It is seen about to leave Workington in about 1953.

The drawbar trailer or 'dangler' was an obvious way of increasing the rigid vehicle's efficiency, this BRS Maudslay vehicle being an ideal example of carrying two awkward fabrications on one outfit. In 1953, 68D28 was part of the Sherwood Group based at Dock Road, Worksop, these premises being acquired from Sergeants Transport on nationalization. The Mark 2 Mogul had a dropside body, the sideboards being removed for this load, then stacked behind the vehicle's headboard. FA 8766 was transferred to BRS Barnsley in 1956, and was renumbered 3D313 prior to disposal on 17 December 1959.

The six-wheeler was also a natural to take advantage of the higher weight limit allowed when hauling a drawbar trailer. George Kirkbright is seen in his own AEC Mammoth Minor which dates from 1937. Kirkbright's were nationalized and recommenced in the 1950s under the name of Peel Transport of Halifax, although still having a base at Colne. They were to operate until 1986, when they were sold out to Potts Transport of Crosshills.

**Above right & right** When seen side by side, the wagon and drag was always to beat the artic both in potential payload area and potential maximum weight. Onward's SWX 412 dates from 1956 and is seen hauling a Dyson drawbar trailer at Templetown about 1962. Rankin's Leyland Beaver is of 1957 vintage and is hauling a Dyson built semi-trailer. Both outfits illustrate a fine standard in the difficult area of roping and sheeting of their loads.

**Left** Scammell offered their own particular version in articulated couplings for maximum weight vehicles which were directly comparable to the versions used on their small mechanical horses. These systems lost out in favour of the SAE-type coupling, which in principle was an import from the USA with their war effort vehicles. Of note in this Eddy Tomlinson photograph are the power-operated automatic landing legs and the almost mandatory warning to the rear concerning air brake fitment. MBU 650 dated from 1955.

**Left and below** Not every articulated vehicle was made as two distinct parts for these examples illustrate two outfits intended very much to remain as a single unit. Both illustrate bodywork by Scammell & Nephew in an era when emphasis on aerodynamics on goods vehicles had never been given much thought. The John Collier outfit dates from 1954, the Leeds Co-op mobile shop from 1959, both being based on Austin tractive units.

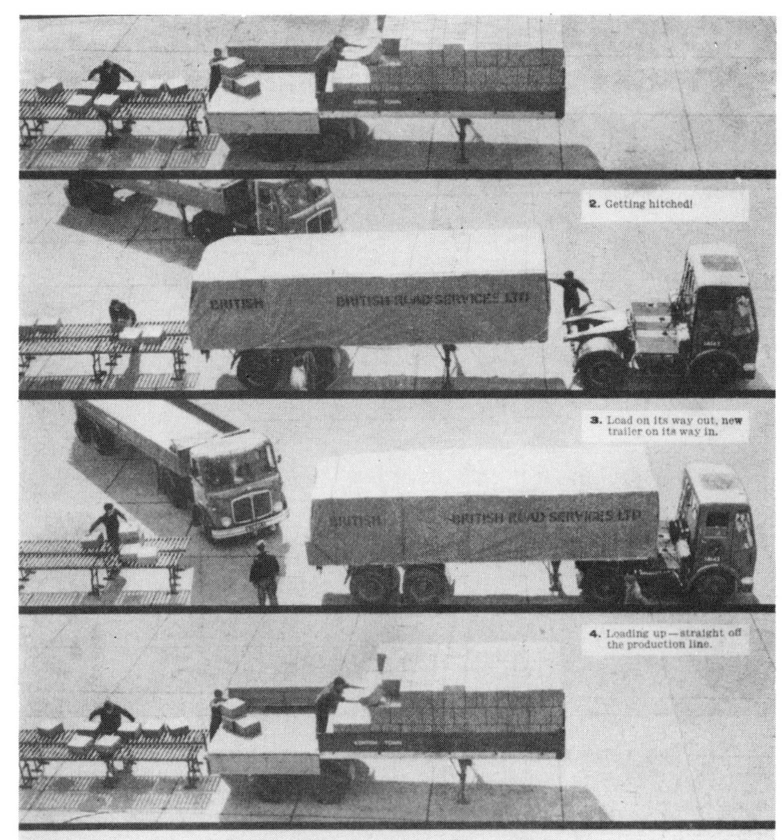


**Right** This original British Road Services advertisement dating from the early 1960s clearly illustrates one of the big advantages of articulation. The tractive units in use are of AEC Mercury and Bristol manufacture.

**Below** The eight-wheeler might not have had the flexibility of the artic but it was certainly a faithful haulage tool. This BRS line up is seen at Workington about 1962. The three Fodens are PTD 992, 991 and 517, with chassis numbers 35094,92 and 68, being produced in March, April and May of 1953 respectively. John Mollett's extensive research records that these three started life as box vans with the BRS Manchester Parcels group. The Leyland Octopus, being third in line, was 635 BTD, fleet no 3C1377, chassis 570411, built in March 1957. It started with BRS as a contract vehicle to ICI Dyestuffs, Kearsley, Bolton being no C2C 5293 until the contract ended in 1961.

**Left** The eight-wheeler was also being used as a platform towards the demand for high-performance goods vehicles as the country entered the motorway era. The small Rolls-Royce badge on the grille of this 1960 ERF is the only outward sign of a petrol-engined vehicle capable of speeds well in excess of 60 mph, yet still producing credible fuel consumption at its 24 ton gross weight.

**Below** The eight-wheeler felt itself deserted almost overnight with the change in law allowing articulated vehicles to run up to 32 tons gross weight. The restrictions in the law initially meant that in practical terms five axles had to be used for this new weight band and the Scammell Trunker II was one of the few tractor units quickly available for this type of work. Sporting the new Arrow logo, MRH 622F was recalled as being a bit of a punishment vehicle by its drivers. Calor Transport ran a number of Trunkers converted with fitment of the pneumo-cyclic, semi-automatic gearbox normally used in the Leyland Atlantean bus.

**Right** With a relaxation in the weight limits, articulated vehicle length limits were also eased to allow standard use of longer semi-trailers. The one obvious disadvantage of this was a loss of strength at certain points although such an awkward load of steel as this, seen in August 1972, would have tested any vehicle. (The name has been blanked out to save embarrassment).

**Below right** Seen in regular use in many other countries, the double outfit or double bottom as it is known elsewhere, has never been generally legalized in this country. Crane Fruehauf, however, with both ERF and Volvo were very active in testing trials during the 1970s, these illustrating that such a concept could be both safe and viable in a geographically relatively small country like ours.

**Below** Of importance in the changing field of carrying cargo was the invention of the Tautliner in 1969, the first load-bearing body with curtain sides. What could have been hours spent on roping and sheeting was transformed into seconds as the curtains were moved into position and tensioned down. Following the launch in October 1969, 20 such trailers were built in that year. This has been dramatically topped by Boalloy producing about 7,500 in the UK during 1985. Tautliners are being built, either under licence or in kit form, in countries all round the world.

**Above** The tilt type of outfit has regularly been favoured on the continent especially for TIR work although inroads into this have been made by the curtainsider. Getting into the side of the tilt has always been a rather lengthy job, although its advantage over the curtainsider was that the roof could be removed if required. AM Garage of Birmingham used this Saviem SM36-380/Crane Fruehauf outfit to maintain a regular supply of spares to Renault Trucks' UK central warehouse.

**Below** Changes were also in store for the front part of the goods vehicle, and although the Foden half cab was normally seen as a dumper fitment, Fred Robinson ran quite a number of these on his night trunk between London and Teesside. Fred argued that as well as being cheaper than a full cab, they not only cut down on unauthorized passengers, but also assisted with increasing access to the engine compartment without having to remove the fixed cab.

**Above** The tilting cab is now commonplace, but it should not be forgotten that George Neville first championed the concept as early as 1944. George failed to interest any of the big names and only a few of his 'tipping' cabs were made. Once his patents had expired, people like Foden were to develop their own similar idea. Of particular note in this Arrow Bulk photograph of the Easthaugh Bros liveried Foden 26 ton gross eight-wheeler is the long wheelbase, the fire-screen behind the cab and the fine balance in tanker construction.

**Above right** The deep proportion of the sleeper cab was the next step, although finding this type of vehicle in the Robson fleet used to be a rarity. The late Stan Robson felt that once a driver had done his day's work he should spend his rest period elsewhere than in his cab. Seen loading in Carlisle, *Border Hunter* is chassis number 257589, first registered in Nov 1984.

**Right** The rigid never had the free space available for normal fitment of the sleeper cab although mounting it above the day cab as in this Perfecta Bedding outfit could also enhance the general aerodynamics of the vehicle. Perfecta operated four of these M16 ERFs fitted with the Gardner 6LXCT engine, which gave fuel consumption between 11 and 13 mpg. The outfit illustrates the rigid alternative to the artic being fitted with an Abel demount system for the Vanplan bodies, and centrally mounted axles on the Primrose drawbar trailer to assist in manoeuvrability.

# 2. Drop in, tip out

If there is one type of cargo carrier that is always able to conjure up a variety of thoughts to a variety of people, then it must be the tipper. Its image has for many years tended to portray a dirty, rather unkempt vehicle, always slightly older in years than most, making more noise or belching out more smoke than any other vehicle. When empty the tipper always seemed to be able to go faster than most lorries on the road, the rattle of its large flimsy body an undisguised signal of its approach. When loaded the tipper seemed the slowest vehicle ever to be invented, always close to collapse under its highly piled payload.

Perhaps this image had something to do with the way it deposited its load. True, this was normally in a heap, but it was generally an ill-defined heap, never really tidy. But in being able to throw his load from his back, the tipper man always had the last laugh on his platform-bodied counterpart who could spend hours slowly lifting off his load piece by piece.

The concept of the tipper is really as old as the trusty horse and cart. The early tippers simply made the horse reverse, and with the wheels of the single-axle cart held static the movement saw the body try to rotate around its axle and thus the cart's contents were tipped from its rear.

For even longer tippers an ingenious device was conceived which also relied on basic physics and the principle of moments. The body of these extra large tippers was made so that half of its length was supported on the cart proper whilst the other half of the body projected from the rear of the vehicle as an overhang. The body was made to hinge around its centre, which coincided with the rear of the cart chassis, but it was held secure by a stay which locked the body into a horizontal position. With the tipper evenly loaded and the discharge point reached, the securing stay was simply knocked out, allowing the body to rotate about its hinge. This angular movement would be aided by applying hand pressure to the rear of the body, but once the load started to slide out nothing could prevent it from being discharged.

Utilizing a modern-day system operating on that principle would obviously save a great deal of expense on costly tipping systems, but unfortunately the law soon outlawed the general principle of having this 100 per cent overhang on lorries, believing it to be too dangerous an imbalance for general road safety.

The ability to unload your vehicle in one single movement may have been quite a boon, but getting the load on to your vehicle in the first place was always a different proposition. It is all too easy in this modern day of mechanical aids, such as highly-adaptable loading shovels, to forget that the early operators normally relied on a shovel propelled by manpower to throw the cargo on board, although there are still a few people around who can remember.

R. Durham & Sons is one of the biggest general hauliers currently operating on Teesside, where founder Bobby Durham started off with a pony and cart in 1922. In 1936 he got his first Bedford tipper used for the door-to-door delivery of sacked coal. Purchased at the equivalent of 87½p per ton from Bowburn Colliery, the coal was retailed at 6¼p a sack, although buying in bulk saw the price of five sacks on sale at 30p.

Bowburn, like many other pits, was strictly limited in its overhead loading facilities, so the rules were that all the tippers present at 6 o'clock in the morning were put into the hat and a draw made for preference of loading. Those that were lucky enough had their tipper bodies filled with coal by means of the overhead chute, but if your name was not drawn out, or perhaps you were slow in getting out of bed in the morning, then you had to hand-load your vehicle all by yourself.

Even the first tipping gear demanded a great deal of physical effort, as the basic mechanical system operated like some current car jacks. A side-mounted handle was meshed through intermediate gear wheels, so that on turning the handle a fixed rack mounted to the body of the tipper would be rotated upwards and thus lift the body. The body was hinged at the rearmost point of the chassis, the point about which those first long hinging tipper bodies had been made to rotate.

Variations on this theme saw threaded screw mechanisms also turn to lift the body, although lowering an empty one was always a lot quicker, because by knocking out the engaging pawl, the force of gravity would bring the body down back to its lowest position. Those who favoured this swift method of lowering also had to remember to move out of the way quickly for fatalities were caused by drivers getting trapped under the falling body.

The tipper was thus an unforgiving type of vehicle apparently destined to spend its life in and out of some of the worst places possible. Coal yards, quarries, spoil heaps, road works: whenever the going got rough you normally would find a tipper ploughing about in it. The general haulage vehicle would stop at the roadside and survey the filthy site. Not for him ploughing in up to his axles to try and get his cargo closer to the drop off point; like a sensitive filly that would sniff the air with disdain, you wouldn't get it dirty like that. The tipper was more of a hack. Heavy-footed drivers would tear the heart out of the lead-footed vehicle forcing it through conditions it shouldn't really have to bear, for the men involved on this side of the business were always a little bit on the hard side.

A story is told of one tipper boss going round his yard one Saturday morning passing the time of day with the men. Nobody got overtime to work on a Saturday, it was just expected that you came in to do your own servicing. The boss met up with one of his drivers walking across the yard and he couldn't help noticing that a sole on the driver's shoe was flapping and close to coming off completely. The boss was naturally concerned about this, especially when the driver told him that he couldn't afford to repair his shoes, because he just didn't have the money. Thinking no more about it, the boss put his hand to his hip pocket and pulled out a bundle of pound notes, so many that they had to have a thick rubber band round them to keep them together.

'Here,' he said, 'take this. That should do the trick' and with complete unselfishness he unwound the rubber band, handed it to the driver and told him to wrap it round the sole of his shoe to stop it flapping.

The life of the tipper man certainly became a lot easier with the advent of the hydraulic ram. First these rams were pumped up by hand, but utilization of the power from the vehicle's engine could be used to drive a hydraulic pump. The pressure of the hydraulic fluid was channelled into the ram so by pressurizing the fluid, the ram would be activated to lift the tipper body upwards, once again generally hinging at the extreme end.

This end form of tipper was generally the most traditionally used vehicle but an early concept still in limited use is the three-way tipper, which as the name suggests can either tip to the rear or to either side. The three-way tipper works on a system of four securing mechanisms which also double as body hinges. If, for instance, it is required that the tipper discharges its load to the offside, then the two locks fitted to the vehicle's nearside are released which leaves the two on the offside engaged. When the tipping mechanism is activated, the result of having the two locks/hinges still secure means that the body will naturally rotate about this point and thus discharge to the offside. Tipping either to the rear or to the nearside is thus accomplished by releasing the relevant mechanisms to allow the body to go in the desired direction.

The three-way tipper by reason of its design must be fitted with under body rams which must be given some latitude to float around a bit to do the job they are designed for. Naturally this type of tipper had to be built stronger and thus heavier to withstand the variance in flexing, and although some local authorities find them ideal to work in limited spaces, the three-way is really a rare breed.

Apart from the three-way mechanism, where you have your tipping gear mounted sometimes comes back to personal preference, although trends affecting this locating have changed with the passage of time. Having it mounted at the front of the body immediately behind the cab meant that it was in close proximity to the engine and hydraulic pump driven by means of the pto (power take off). However, it also meant the length of the body was reduced because a space had to be left between the cab and the body for the tipping gears to work in.

Mounting the rams under the body meant you could utilize all the body space available. However, because these rams were mounted more to the centre of the vehicle they had to work that much harder than the front-mounted rams when lifting the same amount of weight. In being completely under the body as opposed to down the side of it, the under-mounted gear tended to hang low beneath the vehicle so making it susceptible to damage by upward projections on a rough site.

The pros and cons could be argued for both systems, but the modern trend is towards front-mounted single rams of massive strength and reliability. Twin rams were certainly well favoured in the past, but their big drawback was that if they did not work together in exact harmony, then the one working the hardest would try and push the whole body both upwards and sidewards, thus inducing a roll over.

Instability has always been the tipper nightmare. It never really bothered the early vehicles for these tended to be small in nature, generally at work on local hauls only. Small bodies on short wheelbases could discharge their load almost as quick as you could open the tailboard. But the expansion in trade and industry during the 1950s made the 5 ton tipper close to redundant. The six and eight-wheeled rigids were put into use, generally of a shorter wheelbase than their platform counterparts but still able to carry a good 15 and 16 tons within the 24 ton gross limit.

It was naturally more efficient to use one vehicle rather than three or four little ones so when that gulf was created with the introduction of 32 tons for artics, the tipper men dipped their toes into waters they had never looked in before and considered the unthinkable prospect of an articulated tipper.

The tipping fraternity is strange. They subject their vehicles to the greatest abuse so far as operating conditions are concerned yet their general rates of payment for payload moved have always seemed the lowest in haulage. Thus they require a vehicle which is as strong as an ox but at the same time is as light as possible to carry the maximum amount of payload. The latter pressure on fee earning made the artic more presentable.

It is true that trends in the tipping game were changing. The late 1950s and 1960s saw the long distance tipper man become more of a regular breed. Econofreight on Teesside, now well known for heavy haulage, ran a large number of Atkinson eight-wheeled tippers to all parts of the country carrying products like dry chemicals in bulk. The multi-wheelers with extensions on their body sides known as 'greedy boards' were also growing in popularity for carrying coke, so why couldn't the artic make a contribution in this area of transport? The temptation was too great to turn aside and in the 1960s the artic tippers came in a flood, the thought of roll overs pushed aside.

It wasn't just at the delivery point that concern was felt about discharge, for, as Bruce Rowbotham recalled, the tipper problem could hit you anywhere.

The Albion five or six speed gearbox is a joy to use although when they wear, the shift from fourth to fifth up the box can mean a long travel of the gear lever from resting close to the engine cover to almost striking the back of the cab. One such tipper driver making that shift was building his speed up as he drove down the A1 at Catterick. What he didn't realize he'd done was that as he had banged the gear lever back into top, he had accidentally engaged the drive for the power take off and thus started off the hydraulic tipper mechanism. The tipper body raised as the vehicle was driving along and all the closed tailgate succeeded in doing was to ensure that all the load was retained right over the rear of the vehicle. The driver realized there was something wrong once his front wheels had left the ground. The tipper eventually came to a halt, quickly spilling its thick tarmac load on to the road. Once outside the warmth of the insulated tipper body, the tarmac quickly congealed into a solid, massive lump.

Years before the invention of the short take off ramp used by the Harrier jump jet whilst on aircraft carriers, some car drivers on the A1 had tried a similar manoeuvre and enjoy the thrill of flight, albeit for only a few seconds. This type of incident apart, the manufacturing of tippers has now become close to a science as builders strive towards greater stability although it could be said that this attitude is long overdue especially with artic tippers. The problem of roll overs is not an isolated one; researchers at Bristol Polytechnic estimated in 1984 that there are probably 900 incidents a year in the UK as a whole.

The traditional rear end tipper is being asked to perform a great deal as dimensions of vehicles and the weights they operate at keep going up and up. Smoother body designs tapering to the rear slung as low as possible have been introduced to aid the swift smooth flow in discharge, but when it is calculated that a 2° cross slope can bring instability, never mind factors like wind direction, a sticky cargo or even a deflating tyre, it is apparent that this problem requires a great deal of urgent research and application.

One man who continues to make a massive contribution in this field is George Neville who even at the age of 75 is still hard at work in his crusade towards safer tippers. The Nevilles are a Mansfield family born and bred, and George is a man who has the gift of being ahead of his time. In the late 1930s the Bedford dealership he ran built up a thriving business of converting the bonneted 'O' series Bedford into a forward control vehicle which thus allowed far longer body space on the same length of chassis. This conversion cost £30 although a de luxe coach-built cab would set you back an extra £15.

During the war, the Nevilles were making producer gas plants which would burn coal, coke or even wood shavings to produce inflammable smoke, a strange method of propulsion prompted due to petrol being virtually unavailable.

In October 1944 George patented his tipping cab or tilt cab as it was to be called 20 years later. Even though it turned heads and rocked the industry when it appeared at the 1948 Motor Show, none of the big truck manufacturers was interested and although many conversions were carried out — more than 12 Bedfords went to Hoveringham Gravels Ltd — the patents were allowed to lapse due to lack of finance to protect them. But it was to be in tipper design that Nevilles were to find their niche.

The company sold out in 1962 due to crippling death duties being levied after the death of George's father, and although George did stay with Neville-Charrold for four more years, his creative urge demanded that he leave and set up on his own again.

In 1977 the Design Council recognized his talent and his award for the 'Easysheet' reflected on the ingenuity of being able to sheet and secure the load without the driver having to leave the ground. Working through a hydraulic mechanism, the Easysheet could sheet and unsheet itself in a total time of no more than 1½ minutes. It was to be a boon for wagon drivers, although strangely British Rail also recognized the brilliance and gave orders to Nevilles for fitment to a large number of their railway trucks.

1983 was to see the first 38 tonne tipping artics and since then George had produced stabilizing legs for underbody fitment and even championed a new concept of tipping imported from Canada. Currently there is only one Delescope at work on the road although its operator can carry nearly twice the amount of payload of conventional artic tippers in a vehicle which is far less prone to instability.

With a semi-trailer built to the maximum length of 40 ft this seems hard to believe, although discharge from the Delescope is done in two distinct phases. In the first phase the front half of the tipper body slides backwards and by telescoping itself into the rear part of the body, it discharges most of the load in this fashion. A conventional tipping ram is then used to discharge what is left, but because this only involves virtually half the load the problems of stability are thus cut in half.

Another exciting concept in the tipper field concerns both its manoeuvrability and off-road performance, although the use of the Multidrive was only allowed after the law was changed to allow this brilliant concept on the road. Visually they may appear like any other articulated tippers, but the prototypes headed up by Leyland/Scammell four and six-wheeled tractive units are the pioneers of an entirely new idea in goods vehicle. The idea was conceived by David Brown, the son of the David Brown well-known for DJB dump trucks. Multidrive Ltd based at Peterlee, County Durham, in co-operation with Crane Fruehauf and Leyland, have produced a vehicle which turns the believed principle of articulation completely on its head.

What Multidrive have done is to take the drive through the drive axle of the tractive unit to the trailer bogie by means of a special three-piece propeller shaft. The normal semi-trailer running gear has been replaced by a conventional double drive bogie from the Leyland Constructor 6 × 4 and 8 × 4 rigids. The Multidrive is in essence either an 8 × 6 or 10 × 6 (depending on the number of axles on the tractive unit), although its amount of articulation has to be limited to protect the through propshaft's universal joints from extreme angles. In fact the conventional fifth wheel coupling has been replaced with a much stronger type of turntable of the sort normally used on drawbar trailers, so in some respects this vehicle is very much a rigid which just happens to bend in the middle. A similar turntable is mounted on top of the trailer bogie which is also steered by two crossover rods that are connected to the tractive unit in the area of the foremost turntable mounting.

The concept of the Multidrive has revolutionized both the artic and the role it has to play in the tipping game. It is just as well that such developments are getting to grips with some of the problems that have beset this type of vehicle, for it now finds itself being utilized in an area of transport that started moving fluids but is now the scene of great diversification.

**Left** This S-type chassis was made by Foden in 1933 although its clean lines would still be appreciated by tipper men of today. The vehicle is in fact an example of the three way tipper, the front offside securing/hinge mechanism clearly visible. The fine print on the side of the Dorman-engined vehicle gives an unladen weight of 3 ton 18 cwt 2 qr, which is just below the tax concession figure at that time of 4 tons.

**Left and below left** Talk to some old Foden followers and they will tell you that the DG series introduced in the mid-1930s was the finest vehicle around at that time. Tipper operators found that the vehicles were strong and could take a fair percentage of overload in their stride. Both these Peak District vehicles sport three-way tipper mechanisms. The six-wheeler tipped the scales at 7 ton 5 cwt and dates from 1938; the eight-wheeler dates from 1946.

**Above** With such a strong reputation, the Foden DG was a natural for internal and off road applications, this six-wheeler having an obvious air of confidence about it as it is seen prior to leaving the works. One drawback of the underbody tipping gear is that in the lowered position, the telescoped rams hang down below the main chassis frame. To afford protection for the mechanism, an underslung front bumper is fitted to snowplough upward projections out of the way.

**Below** For assured discharge on rough or unstable ground, the bottom dump vehicle is a far safer proposition. This Euclid-built semi-trailer operates its two side hinging doors through cables driven by the mechanism on the trailer rear nearside wheel. The bottom opening of the doors thus allows the contents to fall to the ground without having to tip the body. Euclid did offer their own tractive unit, normally through Blackwood Hodge, so it seems strange to have this modified Thornycroft Antar for such an application.

Frank Annis may have been famous in the heavy haulage circles, but he was also an early mover of cement and gypsum in the London area with vehicles like BBK 528, an enclosed tipper of 1938 vintage.

The Cement Marketing Company also used a variation of vehicles for bulk movement of cement. 1086 was one of a large batch of dual-purpose vehicles, registered NXW 787 in 1953. Discharge from the bulk body was by means of under ram tipping gear, although the vehicle's design allowed for the bulk body to be removed (it was attached by a system of clamps) and bagged cement carried on the platform. The only operational drawback to this system was that the relatively short wheelbase, ideal for tippers, was never long enough to carry the maximum weight of bagged material.

In general the early tippers were mainly four-wheelers, with Glendenning's ETY 307 being a 1951 example of the highly popular S-type Bedford. This model was first announced at the 1950 Commercial Motor Show, powered by the 4.9 litre petrol engine producing 110 bhp. Diesel-powered S-types were to be offered from 1952 which ensured the popularity of the big Bedford until it was superseded by the TK range in 1960.

**Above** The role of the tipper saw it destined for places that no other lorries would go, this trio of Wynns vehicles being nonchalantly engaged in filling in a timber float at Newport Docks. The gear on the tipping Guy Otter consists of a powerful short stroke hydraulic ram lifting the body through a shaped lever attachment. Wynns had two Otter tippers, fleet numbers 274 and 275 being registered PDW 849 and 850. The small Drott machine is driven by Courtney Evans.

**Below** The problems of working on site should never be forgotten. The Euclid 15 ton dumper tried to get too close to its drop off point whilst the O series Bedford was always too wide for a narrowing gap. An entirely unconnected incident recalled by Roger Elsom saw two Foden tippers collide head on with each other. Both were only a week old and both were driving in opposite directions along a stretch of aircraft runway of an old RAF station that was being cleared by a sand and gravel merchant. The mind finds difficulty in understanding how they crashed together.

**Above** The big name in sand and gannister of the 1950s and '60s working the hills of north west Durham was Redmires of Wolsingham, the company being owned by the Ward family. Truck followers in Consett will never forget the sight and sound of these eight-wheeled Fodens that kept Consett Iron Company going with the special raw materials it needed for fine steel production.

**Below left** Also worked in north-west Durham was this Chinese Six of Glendennings. Just bought second-hand from Peter Slater, Gildersome, West Yorkshire, the Leyland was remembered for its ineffective handbrake, whilst the tyres are also seen to be needing attention. Maximum use of space has been made by building the body forward to enclose the end tipping rams.

**Below right** Another way of increasing body size regularly used on tippers was 'greedy boards', with which the sides of the body were extended upwards. They are clearly visible on this BMC four wheeler in 1962. The novel ramp mechanism, not particularly strong but still very effective and still in use 25 years after this photograph was taken, allows for unassisted transfer of the load of lime prior to it being spread on the adjacent fields.

**Above** Used mainly on local or internal movements around ICI at Billingham, this AEC Mandator-headed tipper (inset) includes a concept that led to an eventual Design Council award. In 1974 ICI approached George Neville for help with some form of mechanical covering system for their tippers, and three years later his 'Easysheet' method won the acclaim it deserved. Another sign of stress on the hard-worked tipper is illustrated in the Dennis Harris photograph (main picture), as close to 10 tons is being dropped on to its back from a very great height. The Crane Fruehauf semi-trailer carries its own independently-driven donkey engine so that the tipper mechanism can be powered without the need of a tractive unit power take off. The Seddon Atkinson 400 unit of Sandersons of Great Broughton normally hauls platform trailers on general haulage, the 5½ ton trailer belonging to the parent company of R. Durham & Sons.

**Right** Trailer-makers Crane Fruehauf of Norfolk pride themselves on the strides they have made towards greater stability with the articulated tipper. In 1985 they were to claim that their latest 38 tonne artic could lean further sidewards before the chassis threatened to bend than a comparable 30 ton rigid eight-wheeler. This CF 1987 model has a step frame supporting the alloy body on air suspension.

**Left** The eight-wheeled rigid continues to be a solid representative in the tipper game. John White is one of about 20 other owner drivers working a 40 mile radius out of Raisby Quarries near Coxhoe. John is more than happy with the performance from the 300 bhp Caterpillar engine although at 6½ mpg he accepts it is a bit heavy on fuel. Seen depositing a load of wet mix — limestone that's been wetted to make it easy to roll out — the Stanley-made body with air-operated tail gate is being lifted by an Edbro ram.

**Below** Mercedes-Benz have established quite a following in the UK tipper business, this 3025K model being the fourth Mercedes to join the 14 strong tipper fleet of Leith's Quarries. Used to deliver dry and coated roadstone in north-east Scotland, the vehicle is fitted with an insulated aluminium body built by Eric Paton of Netherley and twin ram underbody tipping gear.

**Above** With high profile companies like Knowles of Wimblington, the image of the tipping business can only be improved. These nine Volvo FL10 6 × 2 tractor units coupled to York Big Chief semi-trailers were a big investment to the haulier who put them on the road for the new E prefix in August 1987. Used mainly for bulk grain and animal feed movements, the bodies are lifted by Edbro single ram tipping gear.

**Below left** The Delescope concept imported from Canada seems to have quite a lot going for it. Although not stated on this brochure, the sole operator of this type of vehicle in the UK uses the sliding body principle to compact his load prior to moving off and thus can carry up to 22 tons of paper-type material, nearly twice the weight that a conventional artic tipper can move of the same product.

**Below right** The specification of the Multidrive has allowed the use of the articulated type of vehicle in situations where even a double-drive rigid eight-wheeler would have thought twice.

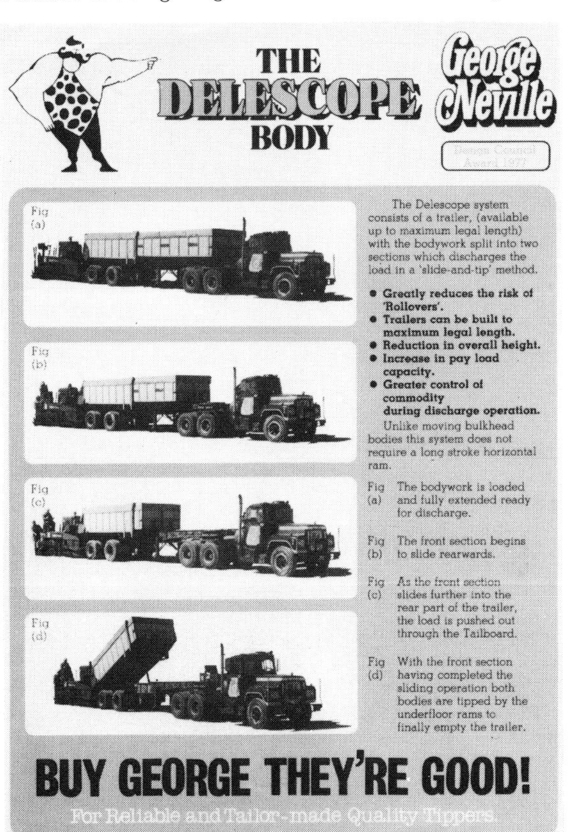


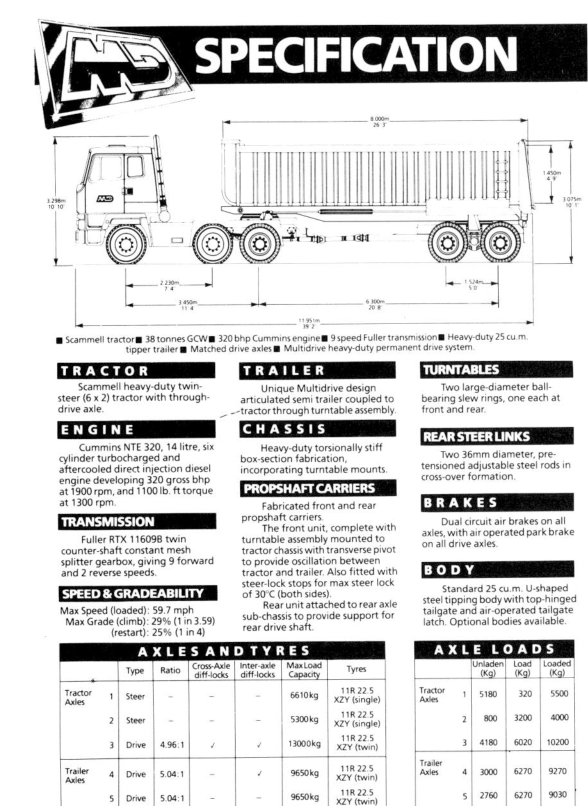

SPECIFICATION

8.000m 26' 3"
1.450m 4' 9"
3.298m 10' 10"
3.075m 10' 1"
2.230m 7' 4"
1.524m 5' 0"
3.450m 11' 4"
6.300m 20' 8"
11.951m 39' 2"

■ Scammell tractor ■ 38 tonnes GCW ■ 320 bhp Cummins engine ■ 9 speed Fuller transmission ■ Heavy-duty 25 cu.m. tipper trailer ■ Matched drive axles ■ Multidrive heavy-duty permanent drive system.

**TRACTOR**

Scammell heavy-duty twin-steer (6 x 2) tractor with through-drive axle.

**ENGINE**

Cummins NTE 320, 14 litre, six cylinder turbocharged and aftercooled direct injection diesel engine developing 320 gross bhp at 1900 rpm, and 1100 lb. ft torque at 1300 rpm.

**TRANSMISSION**

Fuller RTX 11609B twin counter-shaft constant mesh splitter gearbox, giving 9 forward and 2 reverse speeds.

**SPEED & GRADEABILITY**

Max Speed (loaded): 59.7 mph
Max Grade (climb): 29% (1 in 3.59)
(restart): 25% (1 in 4)

**TRAILER**

Unique Multidrive design articulated semi trailer coupled to tractor through turntable assembly.

**CHASSIS**

Heavy-duty torsionally stiff box-section fabrication, incorporating turntable mounts.

**PROPSHAFT CARRIERS**

Fabricated front and rear propshaft carriers.

The front unit, complete with turntable assembly mounted to tractor chassis with transverse pivot to provide oscillation between tractor and trailer. Also fitted with steer-lock stops for max steer lock of 30°C (both sides).

Rear unit attached to rear axle sub-chassis to provide support for rear drive shaft.

**TURNTABLES**

Two large-diameter ball-bearing slew rings, one each at front and rear.

**REAR STEER LINKS**

Two 36mm diameter, pre-tensioned adjustable steel rods in cross-over formation.

**BRAKES**

Dual circuit air brakes on all axles, with air operated park brake on all drive axles.

**BODY**

Standard 25 cu.m. U-shaped steel tipping body with top-hinged tailgate and air-operated tailgate latch. Optional bodies available.

**AXLES AND TYRES**

| | | Type | Ratio | Cross-Axle diff-locks | Inter-axle diff-locks | Max Load Capacity | Tyres |
|---|---|---|---|---|---|---|---|
| Tractor Axles | 1 | Steer | – | – | – | 6610 kg | 11R 22.5 XZY (single) |
| | 2 | Steer | – | – | – | 5300 kg | 11R 22.5 XZY (single) |
| | 3 | Drive | 4.96:1 | ✓ | ✓ | 13000 kg | 11R 22.5 XZY (twin) |
| Trailer Axles | 4 | Drive | 5.04:1 | – | ✓ | 9650 kg | 11R 22.5 XZY (twin) |
| | 5 | Drive | 5.04:1 | – | – | 9650 kg | 11R 22.5 XZY (twin) |

Matched drive axles with hub reduction on tractor and trailer with Multidrive permanent all-wheel drive and steer system on trailer axles.

**AXLE LOADS**

| | | Unladen (Kg) | Load (Kg) | Loaded (Kg) |
|---|---|---|---|---|
| Tractor Axles | 1 | 5180 | 320 | 5500 |
| | 2 | 800 | 3200 | 4000 |
| | 3 | 4180 | 6020 | 10200 |
| Trailer Axles | 4 | 3000 | 6270 | 9270 |
| | 5 | 2760 | 6270 | 9030 |
| Total (Kg) | | 15920 | 22080 | 38000 |

# 3. Liquids, powders and gas

If ever there was an example required to justify the expression 'Necessity is the mother of invention', then one should look no further than the thousands of tankers daily plying the road, hauling every imaginable form of liquid, powder and gas.

The road tanker was in fact first produced merely to meet an insatiable thirst for petroleum by the rising popularity of the motor car. It was just plain common sense that prompted the thought 'Why deliver fuel in 50 gallon drums on a platform back lorry, when you could deliver 1,000 or even 2,000 gallons in a purpose-built road tanker?' The obvious retort to this was that there was nothing to deliver it into, but once storage facilities had been constructed, the role of the road-going tanker was clearly defined.

Thompsons of Bilston in the Midlands had built up a high reputation in the construction of static tanks, so producing on a smaller scale was never to be much of a problem. In 1922, Scammell Lorries of Watford also identified the need for this specialist road vehicle, so by working in collaboration these two companies were to produce some of the finest tankers ever made.

All road tanker builders had several problems to solve that were particular to carrying liquid in bulk, in particular the hazard of surge and of course the difficulty in discharge once you had got the liquid on board.

The problem in surge was best illustrated by studying the horses and carts — rullys as they were known — operated by the British Oil and Cake Mills in Hull. This company specialized in crushing a variety of nuts and seeds to produce specialized oils that were shipped all over the world. Their rape oil was bought in massive quantities by the British railway operators for use in their oil lamps because when it burned it didn't smoke or fume. These qualities were also appreciated by the churches who used a similar product called Sanctuary Rape Oil.

Although these oils and other by-products eventually left Humberside in drums, internal movement amongst the 16 mills in Hull was undertaken by 85 shire horses, the pride and joy of chairman Edwin Robson. Some horses were specially adept at moving the 15 ft long, 3 ton capacity oblong-shaped tank rully, but even these massive movers at times were pushed to their knees as the force generated from the surging liquid was clearly illustrated. The fitment of internal plates of baffles was soon identified, although even today road tankers are notorious for clutch wear as the fickle movement of this cargo takes its toll on the vehicle's transmission.

Surge had in fact been kept in reasonable control in the early petrol tankers because fairly quickly the law-makers had identified that in moving such a volatile product, tight restrictions must be placed on the vehicle's construction and operation. The rules included mandatory fitment of a fire screen at the back of the cab, special requirements relating to the vehicle's electrics plus a limit as to how much petrol could be carried in one compartment. In practice this meant that the early artic petrol tankers had anything up to six individual compartments, which as well as compliance with the law did mean that internal movement of this liquid was greatly reduced.

The discharge of petroleum spirit from the road tanker was also covered by law and could only be done using the force of gravity. This in turn meant that all the storage facilities at garages and filling stations had to be located beneath ground level to allow the road vehicle to unload.

Whilst gravity discharge may have been sufficient for a free-moving substance like petrol, it didn't suit other products like bitumen which was also in great demand by the road construction industry. Loaded whilst boiling, bitumen was still rather sluggish to discharge so although road tankers in general were built on the vehicle chassis in such a manner that they sloped towards the rear discharge pipe, something else had to be used to encourage the movement outwards. This was also needed for other products like heavy fuel oil which did not have the restrictions of petrol, and which generally was stored in tanks well above ground level.

To meet this need the tank-building industry devised two entirely different methods of discharge which are still the basic forms in use today. The pump discharge, as its name suggests, utilized a pump driven via the vehicle's engine through a power take off which sucked the product out of the tank then pushed it along the delivery pipe to the storage point. One disadvantage of this method of discharge, especially with artic tankers, was that a lengthy jumper hose had to be utilized. This linked the discharge pipe at the rear of the tanker to the pto-driven pump on the tractor unit thus meaning the pulling or sucking action of the pump was that much longer. Cleaning of the internal workings of the discharge pump was also of great difficulty and a great concern if varying cargos were to be moved.

As an alternative the pressure discharge saw compressed air induced into the top of the tank and on opening the release valve the product was simply blown out from the road tanker and down the delivery pipe. This type of discharge was more simple than the pump method although it could only be used on a tanker of round rather than oval construction — due to obvious physics reasons — which had to be built in a more substantial manner to withstand the pressure and obviously with the man hole covers and other fitments requiring good sealing.

The compressors used to pressurize the air were once again driven from the vehicle's engine by a power take off. Memorable to tanker men in the early days was Scammell's own specially-produced compressor generally mounted on the rear of the cab or to the nearside. This was a massive construction, but it could also be reversed and used to create a vacuum for clearing the delivery pipes of the dregs after delivery had been made. It could even be used to load the tanker by sucking.

These early road-going tankers normally built in mild steel were classed as a highly specialized operation with generally only the petroleum manufacturers interested in their regular use. Their restrictive limitations didn't really endear them to road hauliers, but exceptions like Crow Carrying Company, Harold Wood, Smith & Robinson and John Ancliff came to the fore as specialists in this game. Operators licensed before 1968 meant that hauliers wouldn't waste an Open 'A' licence on an under-used tanker so the general growth with these vehicles was via the Contract 'A' licence where the vehicle was on a dedicated contract for one customer only.

Licences apart, the main restriction on greater tanker use was the risk of contamination. With a dedicated vehicle hauling the same product every day interior problems never really arose, but for the operator who wanted to back load with a different product, he was wasting his time and asking for trouble if he couldn't guarantee that both his tank and his hoses were perfectly clean. Tank operators did offer steam/detergent cleaning facilities to each other on a reciprocal basis, but the basic mild steel tank was a difficult barrel to work on.

With an acute shortage of suitable steel, tank builders offered a variation of solutions to the internal problem. Some offered an epoxy resin lining whilst others produced Colclad tankers — mild steel with a coating of stainless steel on the inside. Neither of these options was a great success and many a tanker driver has spent hours inside his barrel scrubbing it out clean. However, with the advent of high quality stainless steel linked to new welding techniques, the road-going general purpose tanker raised itself to the status of a highly versatile proposition. With some discerning operators even demanding a polished interior to the stainless steel barrel, the tanker may have been a big financial investment but it repaid the haulier by being able to carry diverse products ranging from beer to bitumen, chocolate to chemicals, and virtually any other liquid that was to be made.

The diversification of the road tanker saw it undertake a variance in journeys. Once a vehicle that used to be limited to local hauls only, national and international hauls were becoming routine. Products that had to be kept warm were now being carried in tankers that were lagged with insulation or even fitted with an electric blanket inside the double skins of the barrel.

One disadvantage to this new found sophistication was an ever upward limit to the unladen weight of the road tanker, so naturally the specialized hauliers were always keen to leap into the new weight bands as soon as they were announced. The dramatic jump from 24 ton gross to 32 ton in the mid 1960s saw the tanker men desert their favoured rigid eight-wheeler — except for specialized traffics —

and plump for artics. The heavy investment in the barrel wasn't lost because tank manufacturers were able to increase capacity by cutting the old tank in half, joining it back together with an extension piece inserted in the middle, then putting it on to a new chassis or running gear. Stretching and refurbishing meant a properly maintained tank could last a haulier's lifetime, although the ever increase in capacity did not always meet with everyone's approval.

The changing role of what a tanker could carry put extra responsibility on to the driver's shoulders. Far away from base he was responsible for loading/unloading and cleaning with the dread of contamination ever present. As if he didn't have enough to worry about, he also had to be part chemist and realize that different products had differing specific gravitys. It is not simply a matter of loading your tanker to the top, for things like acids can be nearly twice as heavy as the same volume of water. It was certainly ideal to use a smaller purpose-built acid barrel for this product but normally it would just be hauled in a standard-sized, general-purpose tank which thus could only be filled to no more than two-thirds of its capacity. The large space at the top of the load, or ullage as it is called, meant that the driving of an outfit loaded in this manner had to be particularly sensitive especially when cornering because the consequence of the increase in movement meant that the tanker could be rolled over completely if not handled correctly.

The movement of acids and other hazardous chemicals became very big business which prompted a fresh look at the tanker's role by those interested in all aspects of road safety.

The one generalization of the road tanker is that although they may vary slightly in shape and size, it is virtually impossible to know at a glance what exactly is inside the tank. Many people like ICI and R. Rankin & Sons had been putting product names on the side of their chemical tankers, especially when carrying acids, so all in the business could accept the concept that distinctive labelling was a very good idea. The now mandatory Hazchem labels were first proposed at a symposium involving all interested parties from the tanker business held at Middlesbrough and chaired by Assistant Chief Constable Bill Ashton during June 1974. London Fire Brigade Officers also had a major input into the pilot scheme, which saw distinctive orange and black labels being used on all road tankers running in and out of Cleveland. The label incorporated a hazard diamond appropriate to the nature of the substance, the name and United Nations code number of the product, the Hazchem action code letters/numbers plus a telephone number to ring for emergency advice.

The visual impact of the Hazchem labels mounted on both sides and rear of the vehicle certainly begs attention, although on first sight it may just seem like a jumble of letters and numbers. However, people having regular use of chemical tankers will know the product being carried at a glance, for to them seeing 2PE 1230 is just like saying methanol. (Truthfully, the way it is remembered is to use the saying 2 Pints of Exhibition (a well-known Newcastle beer) at 12.30 pm.)

It wasn't only liquids that were moved by tanker, as diverse powders ranging from flour to cement gradually left their hessian or paper sacks and were carried in bulk by tanks. The dropping of these distinctive-looking sacks may have been a blessing as George Hall recalled when he was delivering a load of cement to Hull one day.

The Blue Circle Cement logo is one that is now regularly seen throughout the country although its origins were Northern Kent in the late 1800s. Due to the pressures and demands made for quantity and quality in the product, 24 small cement producers got together at that time to form the combine Associated Portland Cement Manufacturers Ltd which now trades as Blue Circle Industries PLC. Their combined products were marketed by the aptly named Cement Marketing Company which used the name Blue Circle as a trademark.

However, as well as selling this type of normally-produced cement, the CMC also bought and marketed cement that was an incidental by-product of chemical producers like Marchon of Whitehaven and ICI at Billingham. A variance in trade names was adopted for this bought-in cement, which was even sold in Blue Circle's own bags, but in essence the cement was identical no matter what was printed on the outside of the bag.

Such were the thoughts of George as he faced one irate customer at a regular drop in Hull. 'I'm glad you've got Blue Circle cement this week,' George was told 'that Pioneer stuff you brought last week is rubbish, you can just take it back'. George didn't think it right that he should comment about that order.

The early use of cement bulkers relied on a

strange property relating to the powder of cement which even dry seems to be a heavy dense material. Once cement is aerated (has air blown through it) it virtually runs like water so making discharge that much easier. Visually these first bulkers just looked like a large box van with the internal belts and air ducts concealed inside the bodywork out of sight. These specially-built carriers did have their limitations, but the current fleet of Blue Circle now utilizes a combination of tipping rams and air pressure discharge to move the cement to some very high storage facilities

The transition to moving any product in bulk meant a greater efficiency in transport costings. Although some powder tanks could in general be made in lighter steel as they didn't have to withstand an enormous amount of discharge pressure, they constrasted greatly with the tankers operated by Calor Transport, who specialize in the haulage of liquified petroleum gas (LPG) and other similar products.

Calor Transport trace their origins back to the traumatic winter of 1947. With many parts of the country, the eastern counties in particular, virtually cut off and goods transport in chaos, Calor Gas Distributing Ltd appealed to PX (Eastern) Ltd for help in distribution. That twist in the fates of the weather was to tie the Peck family of PX (Carriers) Ltd forever with that of Calor. If anything the soon-to-follow nationalization of road transport pushed them even closer together. Although the company specialized in cylinder delivery and collection moving 600,000 standard 32 lb units in 1947, the move towards bulk deliveries saw 75 Leyland Lynx vehicles, ex-war surplus, bought and converted for this type of job.

In 1957 Calor had moved 631 tons in bulk but five years later this had leapt massively to the yearly movement of 106,839 tons in bulk plus in excess of 4 million containers from a fleet size of 261 vehicles being supported by sub-contractors.

The current standard Calor tanker has continued to be something of a heavy weight. Built in $\frac{13}{16}$ in steel plate, its standard requirement is that its payload of liquified gas is carried at a running pressure of 210 psi in the single compartment. It could be naturally thought that this is probably the most dangerous load to carry on the road, but I can bear witness to the phenomenal strength of this type of outfit. Loaded to 32 tons, a driver took a corner too fast and probably liquid surge helped to roll him over on to its side. The impact badly dented the tank but there was no leakage and no disaster, even though the emergency services were on tenterhooks for the five hours it took to clear the road.

Such a hefty construction means that the payload of the Calor type of tanker is only about 50 per cent of its all-up weight, that is able to carry about 19 tons when operating at 38 tonnes gross. Not a lot of paying weight you might think, but people like Air Products and Hydrogen Supplies are lucky if they can carry $\frac{1}{2}$ ton of true gas on their 38 tonne all up tankers. Hauliers using these type of outfits were particularly pleased when the excise licence taxation of goods vehicles was changed from depending on its unladen weight to varying due to its gross plated weight.

Unladen weight, however, was still a major problem, although at least one tank manufacturer was to shake the industry by daring to offer lightweight tankers to haul petrol but built using a type of plastic. M & G Tankers of Lye have long advocated their own answer to weight saving in petrol/fuel tankers with their current offering being a 36,000 litre capacity, six compartment tank built for 38 tonnes operation and made of fibre-reinforced composite plastic. This manufacturer has naturally had to work hard to educate the non-believers that their FRP tank is far better than conventional metal tanks be it in the areas of repair, impact or even fire.

This plastic type of material means that repairs do not require the hot work like welding or flame cutting needed on a metal form of tanker. A double wall, sandwich type construction filled with shock-absorbent, fire-retardent polyurethane foam means that it can absorb impacts rather than buckle like a metal tank would.

Its attitude to fire was tested by the independent body of the Health and Safety Executive. Whereas the test tanks made of steel and aluminium ignited their 750 gallons of naphtha after four minutes, the M & G tank of glass reinforced plastic did not ignite its contents even though it was held in the engulfment fire for 16 minutes.

M & G tankers are now well accepted by the big names in petroleum manufacture, although it is understandable to be confronted by those that still feel uneasy about the use of a plastic rather than a metal type of tank build. Technology hasn't stood still in tank discharge, for now thanks to Drum Engineering pumps are now generally located close to the discharge point and the long jumper hoses have been done away with. Drive to this independently mounted pump is now done by lengthy hydraulic hosing although some operators now prefer a combination of pressure and pump discharge.

Interiors now include a glass type of lining especially for the extra sensitive food products so all augers well for the future of the road tanker industry. Those involved are in a position of being able to offer a vehicle that can carry virtually any type of load: a big contrast to the haulier who first has to find out what the load is and then try and find a vehicle suitable enough to carry it.

It was to be the insatiable demand for petroleum spirit by the thirsty private motor car that triggered large-scale use of the road tanker. Shell's fleet number 59 was chassis number 941 and registered YL 19 when delivered on 10 November 1925. The Scammell-Thompson outfit was rated as a 10 tonner, the elliptic tank mounted on a step frame having a capacity of 2,500 gallons. The smaller tank mounted on the swan neck was to carry an entirely different oil based product.

**Above** But it was to be for the frameless road tanker that Scammell–Thompson were to be more famous with nothing other than the tank's own rigidity bridging the gap between tractive unit and trailer running gear. George Baker's research denotes that fleet number 92 had chassis number 1226 being registered YX 6592 and delivered to Shell on 26 October 1928. The four-compartment tank had a capacity of 2,000 gallons.

**Right** Not every filling station wanted or could accept large deliveries, so for local work of small loads the Shelvoke and Drewry Freighter would have been an ideal type of vehicle. With a top speed of 14 mph, the vehicle was driven by two tram-type levers, one pedal-operated brake and no steering wheel. The Freighter may have looked strange but from this one type of vehicle, SD were to evolve their modern range of vehicles which are firmly established in the local authority type of refuse use.

**Right** Bitumen was another product which benefited from being moved in bulk by tanker, although no tank driver liked bitumen once it had gone solid and congealed into a thick black mass. This Ebano vehicle badged as a Carrimore-Lynx was an example of the outfits sold by the well known trailer maker from 1930 with a Leyland tractive unit. Rather confusingly Leyland were to use the Lynx name for an entirely different vehicle of their own about 1937.

**Left** Although gravity discharge into underground storage was a legal requirement for petroleum spirit, other similar products like heavy fuel oil did not have that limitation and normally ended up in storage tanks above ground. The AEC Monarch of 1949 vintage is maintaining the fuel stocks for this American designed motor grader built under licence in 1955 by Distington Engineering of Workington. The hydraulic ram mechanism adjusting the grader blade ensured it was capable of high precision work.

**Below left** The short wheelbase Scammell-Thompson articulated tankers run by ICI were a famous sight, albeit a regular one, on the roads of the 1950s although KMB 665 dates from 1948. Seen about to unload a solution of caustic soda, the driver is releasing the screwed check valve prior to discharge to the adjacent storage tanks.

**Below** Produced by the Steel Barrel Company of Uxbridge, the ERF C15 hauled a stainless steel tanker of 3,000 gallons capacity on dedicated movement of wine and wine type products. To ensure minimal variation of temperature, the elliptical tank was lagged with 2 in of Isoflex and panelled with aluminium sheeting.

**Above** Lined up on the Newport road, the trio of Wynns tankers illustrates the slight variance in shapes and sizes, although all three share the same downward slant towards their rear discharge pipe. The leading 1956 S-type Bedford, fleet no 237 and registered MDW 298, is a 2,000 gallon general purpose tank. 227 is a 1955 version of the virtual standard Scammell tanker but more of interest is the rearmost 105, a 1940 Scammell registered CDW 935 which required pump discharge from the chassis supported oval tank.

**Above right** R. Rankin & Sons were another company who identified the potential in road tankers and after starting with half a dozen four-wheelers on fuel oil, their Teesside interest grew to a 70-strong fleet. 705 SBB is seen outside their newly-opened Trunk Road depot in 1961. The 680 Power Plus-engined eight-wheeler is recalled both for its high performance and its incredibly heavy steering.

**Right and overleaf top** Scammells continued to be well favoured amongst most articulated tank operators, the 1962 Esso Handyman being coupled to a Charles Roberts tanker for heavy oil movement with air pressure discharge equipment. The Doverstrand Highwayman is an Arrow Bulk contract vehicle for hauling synthetic latex. The July 1964 vehicle was modified 15 months later with the fitment of three line air brakes to allow it to run up to 28 tons train weight, which thus meant a clear 18 tons of payload.

**Below** There are no weight limitations when you haul off the public roads and our airports have seen their fair share of varied tankers. Described as being a Super Pluto, this S20 Foden can carry 6,000 gallons of 145 octane purple-coloured fuel for the DC6 at Prestwick airport. Discharged by an open-ended nozzle, the delivery is approximately 50 gallons per minute, although prior to discharge the bonding wire running from the side of the tanker must be attached to earth out any static electricity. The windows above the conventional Foden cab are to assist with manoeuvring close to expensive aeroplanes.

**Above right** With our larger airports now tending to rely on refuelling via hydrant facilities, the jumbo refuellers tend to be something of the past. However, when the passing Tristar is just in need of a top up of 10,000 or 12,000 litres, there is still a job for the new generation of underslung Thompson-built tankers. This jet engine is run on a fuel which is described as AFTA 2949, a form of paraffin without colouring.

**Right** The movement of liquid or surge inside a road tanker may be impossible to see and difficult to measure, but should never be under-estimated. It was strong enough to roll this vehicle on to its side as the driver attempted to make a sweep turn prior to stopping at the unloading installation.

**Below right** The Hazchem method of labelling for tankers carrying hazardous substances is mandatory, but in 1976 when this MAN–Thompson outfit went on to the road, hauliers like Fearns, who have long specialized in carrying acids and were used to putting the names of products on the tanker, ran a dual type of labelling. A regular optional extra fitted to the side of acid vehicles was a length of Armco-type barrier. This cut down on the amount of potential payload, but it did give greater piece of mind when moving such a hazardous product.

BP
air BP

FEARN
22
Telephone BARNSLEY 84106
FEARN
16-232
TANKERS
DODWORTH
BARNSLEY
ENGLAND
M·A·N
DIESEL
PVH 209P
NITRIC ACID
2P
2032
FEARNS TANKERS LTD. Barnsley 84106

**Left** Having the outward look of a box van, this S20 Foden eight-wheeler had been a 1956 Motor Show exhibit to demonstrate an alternative way of handling dry cement in bulk. Bob Murray was the vehicle's regular driver with his normal run being between Teesside and Blyth, but it is pictured here parked up at John Street Square in Consett in about 1962 *en route* to Marley Tiles at Ebchester. Discharge relied on a system of an internal slope and belting which aerated the cement to make it flow out like water. The method was not totally successful especially if the discharging vehicle was parked facing down an incline.

**Left** The modern-day dry powder/granule tankers are more conventional in shape, relying on either air pressure, tipper or a combination of air and tipping for discharge. Sayers of Newbury have specialized in the dry powder business since 1971, the year they took delivery of their first Scania. The company is now firmly established with that Swedish marque. The GB plates on the 111 are not merely for decoration, as Sayers vehicles travel to Spain and Italy on a regular basis.

**Left** Although Cleveland Tankers do not normally run their outfits on six axles, the current taxation of all goods vehicles offers a big discount on the yearly excise licence if more than five axles are used at 38 tonnes operation. This ERF, along with C426 VAJ, is a rare exception to the DAF predominance in the 65-strong CTL fleet. The tractor has a Cummins L10 290 engine with Fuller gearbox, the general-purpose tanker of 29,000 litre capacity being used for Phenol carriage.

**Above** The double cone tanker known as the banana slopes towards its centre so allowing for discharge at this point. This 1628 Mercedes is one of two 38 tonners used for liquid sugar distribution in Scotland and part of the 15-strong Tate & Lyle fleet based at Greenock. The tank of stainless steel was made by Clayton Commercials and is insulated by glass wool to hold the sugar at a constant temperature of 28°C.

**Above right** Carrying their product at a running pressure of 210 psi, the Calor Transport type of tanker is specially shaped at either end to withstand such an internal loading. The single compartment tank carried on French-built, wide spread running gear is used to carry liquefied petroleum gas and made from steel plate which is over $\frac{3}{4}$ in thick. Such a strong build can actually withstand 315 psi, but it does mean that this 38 tonner can only carry 19 tonnes of payload.

**Right** Probably the lightest road tankers on the road are made by M & G Tankers of Lye in the West Midlands. They use fibre-reinforced composite plastic in the tank, but also keep the weight down by using light alloy sideguards and Alcoa aluminium wheels. The manufacturer contends that in the areas of fire resistance, withstanding impact and general repair, the FRP tank is far safer than a conventional metal tanker.

# 4. Out size, over weight

It is in the field of out-of-gauge loads that the cargo-carrying haulier has been allowed to demonstrate his own flair and imagination. The heavy industrial manufacturer may have won either national or international contracts, but he, like his fellow producers, has relied dearly on the lorry.

It is true that the railways can and do move some very concentrated loads, but the demands of high speed passenger movements on the limited amount of track has meant that 'abnormals' have to be moved either at weekends or at other off-peak times, and at the hint of the slightest delay are simply pushed into a siding to be left for a more convenient time to move further on. Movement by barge on the rivers and canals should not be forgotten and even in the early 1980s some castings of over 300 tons were moved from the North Sea to Doncaster up the waterways, so the eventual road haul to Sheffield was kept to a minimum. But both rail and water hauls are severely limited in their scope by the routes of rail and water links, whereas the road haulier virtually has total freedom, both in the route he carries his load and the way that he does it.

Looking back through the history of haulage it seems difficult to put out-of-gauge transportation into proper perspective. Currently the general run of the mill maximum capacity artic can carry loads of up to 25 tons as a matter of routine. There are many six-wheeled tractors which, when coupled to suitable semi-trailers (which can be hired simply for the haul from the local trailer rental outlet), can carry 50 or 60 ton lumps with consummate ease.

Such a practice has virtually underwritten the need for the specialist heavy haulier whose wealth of experience and massive investment in sophisticated equipment sometimes counts for very little when many producers are simply interested in the bottom line or cost of the move.

However, out-of-gauge moves can certainly test the metal of hauliers, although they generally have a varying attitude towards them. Some wish to do nothing except specials, yet others feel equally strongly that they want nothing at all to do with them. The latter argues that he does not want the hassle, the paperwork, the delays in waiting for a police escort and the constraints on times and speed of movement. The specialist, however, enjoys the test, for certainly in the days of yesteryear moving out-of-gauge loads was a severe examination, both in the equipment used and the techniques of carriage adopted. Today the weights and dimensions may have grown out of all proportion from those moved 50 and 60 years ago, but the men involved today still practise the age-old ritual of mentally crossing their fingers to guard against ill luck, as the specialists stretch their ability to the limits.

The techniques of the pioneers were based on the simplest of principles. The load was put on a trailer which was generally oblong in shape and had a steel wheel on each corner. If the load was longer than normal it was rested on two or, though hard to believe, three similarly-shaped trailers. A drawbar was attached to the leading trailer and the whole combination was hauled by a steam-powered locomotive. If more power was needed, a second, third or fourth steamer was hitched on the front, the principles ensuring movement being as simple as that. The problem of how to reach the destination was in the art and craft of the dedicated drivers, who were able to inspire probably the most unpredictable mount ever to travel the roads.

The steamer certainly looks powerful and awe-inspiring, but traction through steel-shod wheels, even with latter rubber or tracked wheel coverings, was always very limited. It never had enough weight on its front axle, so leaping skyward was a regular occurrence. Steering through a system of loose chain linkages was dreadfully slow in operation, whilst the braking system too required a technique of operation all of its own.

The arrival of KD 9168, the first vehicle capable of carrying loads up to 100 tons single-handed, must have been like entering a new world. The steamer driver required guile, craft and an inbuilt ability to sense a copious supply of water wherever he went. The driver of the newfangled Scammell on the other hand needed none of this flair, so it was natural that the new generation of lorry driver was looked down on by the long-standing steamer men. It is true that the steam-powered locomotive did continue to make a vital contribution in the heavy haulage world up until the late 1940s, but just as the steamer had replaced the multiple teams of horses, so the heavy-weights built by the most famous resident of Tolpits Lane at Watford were eventually to ring the death-knell for the steamer.

The 1950s and '60s were undoubtedly the hey-day for the heavy haulage specialists, as the country struggled back to its feet following the hostilities. But when the weights to be moved were not that excessive, there were many operators who would simply press their own equipment into use, which, with a little imagination, could carry a variety of loads. Notwithstanding these bright ideas, it was still down to the skill of the drivers to deliver their loads, and on difficult terrain their passage was occasionally quite hair-raising.

Philip Braithwaite vividly remembers the antics of the faithful Foden he used to drive for Sunters of Northallerton. With the trusty Gardner 6LW engine coupled to the house-end climbing ability of the Foden transmission there never seemed a steep hill that would beat him, although one load to Spadeadam nearly blotted his copybook.

The rocket testing station situated midway between Newcastle and Carlisle rests on the backbone of England. While it was under construction, many awkward fabrications were hauled from all regions of the country to this desolate part of Northumberland. The roads never seemed any easier although Philip and the Foden were regular visitors, and did not seem to worry too much about being able to deliver their loads. With perhaps a little bit more weight than normal on their back, Philip found himself going for crawler bottom gear whilst midway up a testing incline not far from the site.

Those who have been behind the driving wheel in such a situation will know that it can be a heart-stopping moment. The vehicle was hardly moving as the Gardner was slowing to its lowest ebb. As soon as Philip dipped the clutch the Foden dropped from its upward stance and stopped its forward momentum. Philip pulled the gear-stick back across the gearbox gate and down into the lowest ratio. Pounding that clutch pedal up and down as fast as he could, he still wasn't quick enough and the Foden started to roll backwards.

The mate sitting on the other side of the cab was a helpless spectator. Once the Foden started to roll back the passenger door was opened and the mate had one foot on the door mount ready to launch himself rocket style away. With a runaway, self-preservation is one of the golden rules, but the Foden wasn't ready to give up the ghost yet. With a heart-stopping groan the gearbox finally received the message, and with a mighty leap, forward momentum was restored once again.

The fates may have shone on Mr Braithwaite that day, but not so on his unfortunate mate who being stood in the launching position was simply catapulted out of the cab once the Foden decided to change its direction of travel.

If going up hills was bad enough, many drivers far preferred that direction to going down anything steep, especially when loaded well over the top with an 'abnormal'. Just like their general haulage counterparts, the braking performance of the big boys was still totally inferior to what it should have been. The change in retardation of goods vehicles fitted with air brakes was so harsh in the other extreme, that many vehicles so equipped carried warning signs to their rear. 'Caution — Air Brakes' was the message to other road users not expecting a lorry to be able to stop so quickly but to many this badge was still a bit of a status symbol and people like John Garrett know that the early air brake systems were not as good as they were cracked up to be.

The modern-day air brakes, especially those fitted to heavier vehicles, tend to function through what is known as spring brake units which are generally fitted to most axles on a rigid and all axles on articulated tractor units. The bulbous structure of the spring brake unit conceals a massive coiled spring inside the unit. The built-in energy of this coiled spring is strong enough to lock totally on the vehicle's foundation brakes when worked through a mechanical system of rods or levers.

The first necessity of air in a modern air brake system is to be pressurized at such a level that the coiled spring is itself compressed to release the brakes. Via a graduating type of foot valve, air pressure is also utilized to operate the wheel brakes in a normal way, but any major failure or drastic loss of air means that the inbuilt energy of the springs comes to the fore, failing safe and locking the brakes on automatically.

Articulated semi-trailers rarely have spring brake units fitted as standard, but they normally carry a sophisticated system which means that any loss of air in their lines is sensed and automatically operates the trailer brakes. It can be a bit embarrassing to be driving along when suddenly the brakes bang on because the 'red' line has accidentally unfastened itself, but as John knows that's far better than the other alternative.

He recalls mating Jack Stout, one day down in Nottinghamshire with a load of long piling bars. The AEC Mammouth Major tractor unit was not Jack's normal wagon, and had Albert Lowes, its regular driver, not been on holiday, he would have warned Jack to keep a close eye on the air pressure gauge.

All lorries have their own little quirks or idiosyncrasies that are rarely found on any other vehicle, and the quirk on this particular AEC was that the main pipe from the air compressor to the air tank had an awful habit of occasionally undoing itself. Driving the wagon day in and day out, Albert simply kept an eye on the gauge, and once the air pressure fell from its maximum of about 120 psi he knew that the pipe had come free, so he simply stopped and reclamped it to the compressor.

Not knowing about this little quirk Jack drove on quite oblivious when the air gauge started to unwind slowly from its normal running pressure. Obviously the air pressure was only used up when the footbrake was being operated and descending a winding narrow hill not far from the delivery point, Jack naturally had his foot working hard on that centre brake pedal.

It soon became apparent that something was tragically wrong as the wagon started to build speed up. It was no consolation to the panic-stricken crew to see the little red semaphore-type flag pop up from the AEC dashboard to proclaim the obvious statement, 'Warning, No Air'.

The vehicle was going too fast at this point for the crew to bale out, so Plan B was adopted, and they both began to pray. The AEC took to the fields and Jack's efforts helped to keep the artic going straight, for all long steel drivers know that probably the only thing worse than not being able to stop is if you stop too quickly and the load of steel keeps moving straight through the back of the ever-so-flimsy cab.

Thankfully the AEC came to a halt in a most reasonable manner. The undercarriage and suspension had taken an awful hammering in the cross-country ride, and extricating 30 tons of steel from the middle of a field was not at all easy. Fixing the air brakes was not much of a problem; all it needed was to reclamp that troublesome compressor pipe.

Even though hill climbing and hill descending techniques have improved with the passage of time, the principles of moving specials have hardly changed. The long load specialists like Stevens of Great Ayton and the Cook brothers of Consett rarely let anything worry them, no matter what the dimensions. With the vogue for eight-wheelers arriving, the principles were amended slightly so that the load had one end resting on the platform of your general haulage vehicle whilst the other end of the long load was supported on a drawbar trailer, a specially-made bogie or virtually anything with wheels on.

Stevens did in fact operate a batch of converted eight-wheeled tipper chassis as oversize tractor units, although Septimus Cook and his little Foden four-wheeler *Lady Mary* simply adopted a proven formula when he moved long loads with his pole artic. Mathematics was used to calculate a position one-third of the length of the load from the rearward end. The running gear of the trailer was positioned under the load at this point, with the foremost end of the load, encompassing a span of the remaining two-thirds of the length, being supported on the elderly tractor unit. This formula worked a treat with long steel, ensuring an even distribution, although with concrete beams their delicate construction demanded that the load was supported only at its extreme ends.

For heavier loads the low loader was the outfit to use. It is true that the concept was equally suited to carrying high loads, but in keeping the centre of gravity down and having an ability to allow self-loading for movable plant and equipment, the low loader outfit was the heavy haulier's trade mark. AEC did build some low-slung rigids on eight-wheeled chassis for Norman E. Box, but in essence the low loader was always going to be an artic.

The low loader's design was simple in the extreme and for nearly 40 years it hardly altered, with the graceful swan neck tapering down to the load-carrying platform, whilst four wheels in line supported the semi-trailer at its rearmost end. These large tyres were made to knock out for loading purposes, but this was a difficult job detested by many low loader drivers. It was a massive boon indeed when the concept of removing the neck by means of an inbuilt hydraulic mechanism was adopted on the standard low loader when drive-on access was required to the load platform.

The artic, especially in more modern times, has become quite a versatile heavy haulage machine. But for loads more extreme than usual, the techniques adopted today by the specialists are the same as they have always been; what they do is simply support the load on wheels and pull it by locomotives from one end and perhaps push from the other end. It is probably in this heavy haulage area of road transport that a haulier most depends on his drivers and staff, as they stretch the machines and trailers up to and occasionally beyond their limits, for even today heavy haulage can still be a pioneering business.

The principle of the oddly-named locomotive is like its railway counterpart. It needs to carry ballast weight to ensure that its drive wheels keep a firm grip of the road surface as it endeavours to pull its load. The rail locomotive may have this ballast weight simply inbuilt as part of its massive structure but the road loco has to carry these weights in a large compartment behind the cab. Colleagues of one northern driver used to wonder why his ballasted tractor always wanted a double head assistance from another tractor, up even the most modest of inclines. They only realized the reason why his wheels were always spinning when they looked under the tarpaulin covering to his ballast body. To supplement his not over-generous wage the driver had been selling off the dead weight to a local scrap man, so it was only natural that the tractor couldn't really do its intended job in a proper manner.

It is not, however, just a matter of carrying phenomenal masses of ballast because a tractor must be able to show if it is capable to do the haul. True, all that extra weight will ensure grip, but if the transmission is stretched too far and it cannot vent its frustrated feelings by spinning the drive wheels, then either its clutch will go up in smoke or a half shaft will snap, as even the strongest of tractor units do have their limitations.

In the right hands, however, the heavy haulage machine will perform a multitude of super-human tasks, perhaps only occasionally showing its obvious unease at testing its ability. Mick Gill recalls mating Sunters' old Foden 100 tonner one hot day, and although the 6 × 4 tractor was never remembered as being any form of greyhound, it could certainly pull its weight. The vehicle was fitted with the 8LW Gardner engine, but when put to the test it certainly created sauna-type conditions inside the four-door crew cab.

The Foden rarely faltered, no matter what the terrain, but it should be remembered that hill climbing to the loaded heavy haulier of this era was a nail-biting event. You can't just stop half-way up even the most modest of inclines when you have weights like 150 tons or so behind you; firstly you would never restart from a standstill unassisted with that sort of weight, and secondly the brakes were never good enough to hold you and more than likely the retreat back down hill would be anything but organized. The first instructions that a heavy haulage driver's mate would receive was where the wheel chocks were kept, and how quickly you had to bring them into action when the panic instruction of 'Chocks!' was bellowed from the driver's lips.

Such were the circumstances surrounding the Foden's progress as it clawed snail-like up the hill with the Gardner working hard. It was working so hard that the heat from the engine ignited the thick, quilted engine cover used to soften the noise from the Patricroft-manufactured powerpack.

Realizing that there was no way the Foden could stop, Mick spotted a small stream running down the side of the road. Quick as a flash he grabbed the tea pot from the back of the cab, leapt out into the dyke and as the Foden continued ever upwards, Mick ran back and forth with unbrewed water to douse the smouldering quilt.

The big advantage in using a ballasted tractor-drawbar-trailer configuration is that unlike articulated outfits, coupling the two parts of the combination together was generally a lot easier than worrying if the fifth wheel coupling used on the artic tractor unit was suitable to take the pin mounted on the semi-trailer.

The term 'fifth wheel coupling' seems quite a misnomer, especially if the tractive unit has at least six wheels when the coupling should really be renamed the 'seventh wheel coupling' or something similar. The name appears to have crossed the Atlantic Ocean from the USA when masses of American vehicles were imported to be used during the Second World War. This expression apparently originates from the wagon train days of the west when the cart's spare wooden wheel, its fifth wheel, was stored on top of the leading axle and underneath the cart's body. In this position it allowed the front steering axle to turn in relation to the body so making manoeuvrability that much easier. I am not exactly sure how the vehicle was steered once a wheel had broken and the spare had been called into use.

No such coupling worries for the ballasted tractor hitch. Jaw-type couplings made by Rockinger and Jost would eventually appear, but in the main the massive steel pin through a rearward mounted hole was all that was needed to ensure progress. It was advantageous for the pin to have a threaded nut attached or a clip inserted to prevent the pin leaping out, although some pins fitted to the likes of the Scammell Contractor were so heavy that a rope and pulley mechanism was fitted above the pin to assist in its withdrawal or replacement. With the duplication of the drawbar coupling fitted to the front of the ballasted tractor, the crews could partake in a procedure known as 'pulling the pin'. When desired the tractor could be unhitched, turned round and recoupled so that the drawbar trailer was nosed along its desired course.

As a reflection of the varied companies that worked in heavy haulage, various machines were pressed into use as ballasted tractors. The articulated tractor unit was in fact utilized in this role, because the temporary fitment of a ballast box body on top of its conventional fifth wheel coupling, would broaden the vehicle's utilization even if its wheelbase was always a little on the short side.

Scammells were a regular first choice in the 1950s as locomotives and the Pickfords' fleet of that era abounded with massive variations of the Constructor theme. The opponents of the nationalized concern were remembered for their specials, perhaps none more outstanding than Sunters' sole Rotinoff Atlantic registered RPY 767. From Scotland, McKelvies ran some distinctive S20 Foden 6 × 4 units, whilst South Wales's finest Wynns based their meteoric rise on American tank transporter-based vehicles of Pacific and Diamond T manufacture.

Another well-remembered name of that time used the favoured Diamond T as his flagship, but so drastic were the modifications that Frank Annis adopted that he renamed the two tractors 'Annis' after him. Frank originally set up in business as a scrap-dealer back in 1923 working out of Scrubs Lane in Shepherd's Bush. But with a move out to the memorably named Pump Lane at Hayes, Middlesex he turned his hand to haulage, running bulkers, tankers, general haulage vehicles and his very own distinctive brand of heavy haulage machine.

In 1954 PGX 2 was the first 6 × 4 Diamond T to be converted, and following Frank's love of Gardner engines the T's original Hercules was replaced with a massive 8LW powerpack. The main four-speed gearbox was replaced with a five-speed Mack unit, giving phenomenally-low gearing, a basic requirement with heavy weight traffic.

Frank's flair for converting tractors and trailers wasn't really liked by those who tended to conform and had an ordered existence, but with the arrival of the need for plating and annual testing of goods vehicles, the days of fleets like Frank Annis's were numbered. True, the special type heavyweights were always going to be exempted from the rigorous examination, but that applied to the specials was with regard to their ability to deliver the goods, in an era where the record for the heaviest load moved by road was regularly broken as weights just went up and up.

The ability for the specialist mover to cope with this major increase in demand was linked to a number of important technological happenings, the first of which followed because Britain is an island surrounded by water.

As loads grew larger both in dimensions and weight, it grew more and more difficult to find a suitable cross-country route, especially if you were travelling long distances. Loads had been moved by boat for decades, but in the main the only suitable ships were the deep water vessels which were limited in the number of waterways they could navigate for loading/unloading purposes. The alternative to conventional shipping was simply to launch the load into the water and tow it behind a tug, although this was not recommended for the likes of transformers which didn't really appreciate being saturated with sea water.

However, with the arrival of specialist heavy haulage ships like the Fisher's *Aberthaw* and *Kingsnorth*, what prior to that were virtual back waters became realistic slip-off points to such a versatile vessel with shallow draught. Girder trailer outfits belonging to Pickfords and Wynns were regular passengers on the Fisher boats, although occasionally on dry land these lengthy load carriers were sporting rubber skirts beneath the central frame area. This skirt was one of the fitments needed for use with the air cushion equipment whereby the injection of compressed air into a sealed area between the front and rear trailer bogies had the effect of creating a massive cushion of air. This in turn transferred some of the weight from the trailer wheels and so gave added peace of mind when crossing weak bridges or other susceptible stretches of roadway.

The Fisher boats and the ACE were a major success and a great contribution to heavy road transport. However, these concepts were very specialized and so had little bearing on day to day operations; but not so the modular idea, where trailers and semi-trailers could be simply built up in bits to suit whatever was the requirement.

It is over 30 years since Wynns first imported their flat tops from Scheuerle in Germany, although it is probably the Nicolas marque from France that has championed the modular concept around the world.

The idea of the haulier rather than the trailer manufacturer being able to build or rebuild his trailer in whatever configuration he desired was a terrific boon to all, especially for those involved in moves inside the oil rig construction yards where loads weighing up to 2,000 and 3,000 tons were quite regular. These hauls may have been out of sight of the general public, but in December 1986 the population of the north-west was able to bear witness to one of the biggest hauls ever seen, as Econofreight stretched their lead in the record-breaking field.

The concept of moving the regenerator destined for Shell's Stanlow refinery was the practised idea of placing the load on to a trailer then hauling that trailer by an assortment of locomotives. But even the forefathers of heavy haulage would agree that although the principles hadn't changed since their era, it was only the leap forward in technology that made such a haul possible.

When looked at, the 139 ft long, 51 ft wide, 642 tonne mass appeared to be resting on a single trailer comprising 26 rows of axles. However, that one load carrier was an accumulation of Nicolas bits bolted together lengthways and sideways so that the 416 wheels were all harnessed to work in unison, both in the steering and suspension departments.

With the legal trend currently demanding that weights be spread through more and more axles, the way forward in this area of specialist traffics points to an investment, albeit initially expensive, in modular equipment, which can even be self-propelled.

After more than a century, technology has at last started to give the heavy men what they want, although in an entirely different mode of transport barely 40 years old, technological advances have been in vogue since the first ungainly-looking machines heralded an exciting new era in road transportation.

The pioneers of heavy haulage could naturally feel proud of their talent of moving mountainous loads with the most basic of equipment, and they weren't averse either to posing for the photographer. *Flying Fox* was operated by E. Bendall of Portsmouth and is seen in 1906 hauling a Lancashire boiler. The 8 nhp traction engine, which was new in 1900 and exhibited at the Smithfield show in that year, was built by Wallis & Stevens of Basingstoke. This company were to make their last design of steam tractor in 1927.

**Left** As a form of traction, Foden were equally as respected in the steam age as they are today. This 5 ton wagon of Pickfords had chassis number 4040 and was expected to perform a wide variety of tasks. It is seen here on 11 August 1928 hauling a City & South London Railway trailer car from Stockwell in south-west London. The term trailer car was used to refer to this type of railway carriage which had no electric motors and would be incorporated in the middle of a six to eight carriage train. The City & South London Railway now forms part of London's underground system.

**Centre left** This Currie's trailer seen being shunted at Clarke Chapmans on Tyneside in about 1930 may look particularly basic, but the fact that it could be steered through the drawbar on the front axle was in fact a major advance in heavy haulage design. *Jesmond* was a Class B5 Fowler road locomotive number 8473, new in 1900 and bought by William Bland & Son of Gosforth. The research of Alan Martin shows that from 1921 when road legislation numbering was introduced for this type of vehicle, the Fowler was allocated the number NL 1559. Currie's were to acquire the Fowler from Blands in 1926.

**Below left** With the arrival of the Scammell 100 tonner, heavy hauling was transformed overnight. It seemed incredible that only one vehicle could carry so much weight completely unassisted. Pickfords *Leaping Lena*, BLH 21, was uprated from a 65 tonner to become only the second vehicle able to haul three figures worth of payload. This 11 ft wide, 61 ton stator being delivered to Hull Corporation from C.A. Parsons on 19 August 1938 isn't even heavy enough to show the slightest deflection of the trailer frame. M1679 was to be renumbered M9 before leaving the Pickfords fleet in October 1957.

**Below** When the weights involved weren't particularly excessive, many hauliers pressed into use their own equipment with a great deal of success. Chris Miller is using a Carrimore single axle bogie to support this crane girder, whilst the 4 ton 4 cwt Atkinson has a home-made rubbing plate mounted on its back to allow for a turning movement on the foremost bolster.

**Above** British Road Services also used their diverse equipment rather than hand all the outsize traffic on to Pickfords, with the bogie of this 1948 Maudslay Mogul-hauled load having the look of a redundant lorry's back axle. Seen in Workington about 1953 it might be reasonable to surmise that this load was Scotland-bound. London Scottish head office was at 286, Clyde Street, Glasgow, with other depots at Mount Vernion, Carluke, Motherwell, Holywell, Wishaw, Coatbridge and Maryhill Road, Glasgow. John Mollett's research would suggest this vehicle would have been numbered 63B 322, sold on from BRS prior to 1957.

**Below** The ballasted tractor-drawbar trailer configuration would always look more balanced than a co-opted general haulage vehicle. JUP 926 was a 1948 Mandator, one of a batch specially built for CIC's own work. Normally worked between Consett and Jarrow carrying billets, the 5 ton 3 cwt tractor is seen in 1959 hauling fabricated structures for the Hownsgill plate mill then under construction.

**Left** For heavier weights a six-wheeled tractor unit would be coupled to the four in line semi-trailer. The research of Alan Cundy, Engineering Director of Western Excavating traces X904D back to April 1960 when it was collected new from Fodens by driver Eric Vincent and second man Ted Macey. The S20 Foden-Dyson 60 ton trailer was registered 805 GRL, the tractor being fitted with the Gardner 6LW engine, Foden 12-speed gearbox and hand-operated hub reduction on both drive axles. This low loader was used by Western until 1966, the heaviest load known to be carried being 53 tons of RB excavator. From 1966 until 1987 the Foden tractor unit was operated by Western as a recovery vehicle it then being sold to Steve Boscumbe of St Austell, believed for preservation.

**Left** Even the slightest lowering of a trailer bed could be of great beneficial value as shown in this Teesside Bridge photograph taken on the 10 October 1958. The Perkins engined 0-type Bedford GXW 403 dates from 1944. The hauliers, Freeman, Volkers and Stuart are still currently going strong under the banner FVS, owned by the Preston of Potto family.

**Below** For long load work the pole trailer, often of home-made manufacture, was favoured, especially if the cargo was girders, timber or pipes. BTY 885 dates from 1946, but is seen in about 1949 with the previous owner S. Morton & Sons of Wooler having just had their fleet of 14 vehicles acquired to form Unit D241 of the Road Haulage Executive. The ex-Morton vehicles were transferred to form the BRS Wooler depot at the old premises of Redpath Bros. Fleet no 8D99 identifies the vehicle as part of the BRS Sandyford group with head office in Dunsdale Road, Newcastle-upon-Tyne. The Sandyford group was wound up in 1953.

**Above** But it was in the area of carrying the unorthodox that the road haulier could truly make his mark. Produced from a compilation of various tank transporting trailers, Frank Annis made two of these strange girder trailers. They were purpose-built to carry these odd machines which were described as being used in the erection and firing of the Corporal rocket.

**Below left** The haulier may have made the tools of the trade, but he relied on the ability of his crew to deliver safely their charge. Seen negotiating Bodmin in Cornwall on 1 May 1950, this steel construction is a ship's funnel made in North Shields on Tyneside and destined for Falmouth. The Pickfords crew from Leeds and Birtley negotiated the corner without incident.

**Below right** It was certainly a big help if the load carriers could be contorted round obstructions, although Arthur Mathews driving Wynns *Dreadnought* is making this acute turn look easy. The Crane running gear under those straight girders was the well-used set fleet number 333, and its versatility dramatically changed the capabilities of a haulier. The transformer was one of two, weighing about 120 tons, which were delivered into West London about 1952. The Scammell box tractor pushing is fleet no 210, registered number HDW 43 and driven by Archie Morgan.

**Above** Getting into the soft was a heavyweight nightmare. Wynns' Eric Adams is seen coordinating an assortment of fire power to drag this 60 ton load closer to its final resting place at Winfrith Heath, Dorset. The 1958 Coles mobile crane is hooked up to 265, a Thornycroft Nubian tackle wagon put into service by Wynns in 1959. That in turn is pulling Len Smith at the wheel of Diamond T 185, registered in 1947, EDW 553.

**Above left** Also from 1946, DMW 381 was in fact an articulated tractor converted for use with drawbar trailers by the fitment of a temporary ballast box. Reed & Mallik of Romsey specialized in civil engineering work and expected a lot from their fleet. The Scammell looked well cosseted, however, during the winter of 1965.

**Left** The Diamond Ts have always been of timeless vintage, 3630 DW being more than 20 years old before it was registered by Wynns in 1962. Maurice White is driving the leading T carrying a 54 RB excavator on the Crane girder trailer through Pontypool. 91 is fitted with a Wynns replacement cab and has been re-engined with a Cummins in place of the original Hercules. All up pull-push combination weight would be close to 140 tons.

**Above** It is probably only the characteristic wheel cut-outs on the ballast box that give away the heritage of this Annis-built and Annis-named tractor. PGX 2 was the first one of two converted Diamond Ts built by Frank Annis. Its power is perhaps reflected in the photograph at Wellhall Road, South London. The tractor has just pulled away the king post from the trailer forecarriage, dropping the frame of the trailer on to the road.

**Below** Frank Annis also excelled in the production of trailers, with this Annis float having a 60 ton capacity through its eight large tyres, in the days when the law allowed weights up to 11 tons per wheel for abnormal load carriers. The base of the trailer is from a Pacific tank transporter, supported at either end by Dyson running gear. Registration LLL 92OD belies the true age of this 1956 Scammell, which has undergone an Annis rebuild, including the fitment of an eight-cylinder Gardner engine.

**Above and above right** Although heavy loads have always needed stronger equipment, lengthy cargoes can be carried in a variety of ways. Steel Transportation of Leeds, as their title suggests, specialized in carrying steelwork but the 70 ft long fabrications on the 1958 Atkinson would have needed particular care by its driver to maintain their balance. The Thornycroft Trusty illustrates how to carry the 85 ft long main jib, two back stays and two spreaders of a Scotch derrick as seen in the background. Howard Nunnick's research tends to suggest that the term Scotch followed from Henderson's of Glasgow, one of the makers of this type of lifting mechanism.

**Above far right and right** It is probably safer to accommodate your load as much as possible on the entirety of the vehicle, the Kaye Goodfellow S60 Foden making easy work of this 8 ft wide column supported on a 60 ft long Boden trailer. The Clarke Chapman outfit illustrates how to increase the length of your long load outfit and still stay within reasonable bounds. The Leyland Badger tractive unit was a special version of the similar Beaver yet over half a ton lighter in unladen weight. The Power Plus 600 engine was fitted as standard and driving an Eaton two-speed axle through an AEC overdrive top gearbox, the Badger was quite a flyer, able to reach a wind-assisted 70 mph.

**Right** Getting the best of both worlds is the trombone or extendable semi-trailer which can be adjusted to suit a wider variety in lengthy loads. This special order move undertaken by Stillers of Middleton St George was apparently done by the only outfit in the UK which could deliver these particlar 90 ft aluminium roofing strips. Pat Barnes was driving YHN 393Y, the DAF 2800-Nooteboom outfit, which did the local haul at Corby in 1985.

KAYE GOODFELLOW
WREXHAM
MANCHESTER
GLASGOW
KAYE GOODFELLOW
RNB 721J

ENGINEERS

STILLER
TRANSPORT
STILLER
STILLER

**Left** With a strong enough load, the cargo could simply be supported at either end, whilst even with fixed axles on the bogie steering could still be achieved by chaining the bogie drawbar up to the overhead load. This Les Prudden photograph was taken for Dow Mac Concrete in October 1975. The 50 tonne post-tensioned footbridge beam was leaving Tallington for delivery to Spalding Urban District Council. The ERF tractor was specially built for Dow Mac whilst the King bogie is still currently in use by Stillers.

**Below left** Having a bogie which could be steered might at times be advantageous, at other times it might just be a plain liability. Constable Geoff Colling makes a note of the situation, his patrol car being the Austin 2200 which was a six cylinder version of the land crab Austin 1800 saloon.

**Below** Using two steerable bogies McKelvies' weathered S20 Foden 6 × 4 special is close to the end of an eventful haul ending up at C.A. Parsons on 5 March 1963. Getting the crane girder to Tyneside might have been difficult but getting into the works to commence lifting weights in the region of 300 tons required a lot of patience and a great deal of skill from the Scottish crew.

**Above** This may look like a crane and even when built by Leo Gottwald of Dusseldorf, chassis number 183004 was probably modelled on the similar seven-axle mobile crane chassis. Type AMK 400 is in fact carrying a large telescopic boom built for Hewden-Stuart Group in 1982, which is accompanied by sister vehicle EWY 19Y for that vehicle in turn to perform Herculean lifting operations. All up weight of EWY 20Y is 84 tonnes.

**Below** The modern-day low loader has come a long way from its old four in line ancestor. This tri-axle Taskers has a detachable hydraulic swan neck so allowing for easy access to and from the carrying deck. The Morgan Marathon seen on 22 January 1981 is more of a rarity. It is chassis number 001 and built as a prototype at Guy Motors, Wolverhampton prior to the launch of the then new Leyland range.

**Above** As the weights of girder outfit loads went through the 400 ton gross barrier, axle weights in consequence were well in excess of 30 tons a line and thus became a big concern to highway engineers worried about weak stretches of road. The concept of air cushion equipment was devised to introduce compressed air into the manufactured skirt beneath the centre of the trailer. Operation of this meant that when activated the axle loadings were reduced to about 20 tons a line, as the weight was spread down the vehicle's length. One disadvantage of the first cushion system — ACE 1 — was that the rear pushing tractor had to be unhitched to allow the blower truck into position. Tommy Cromwell is seen in 192 *Dreadnought* at Manchester in February 1967 hauling Wynns trailer 789.

**Below** It was only natural that with the increase in weight the heavy hauliers were obliged to consider alternatives in transport when the traffic had to move considerable distances across the country. The two Fisher boats *Aberthaw* and *Kingsnorth* were specially made to assist with movements for the Central Electricity Generating Board. Their loading link span and deck could be angled to meet their oncoming charge, although even with a shallow draught, use of the vessels was still at times dictated by the state of the tide. *Kingsworth* is winching on Wynns 48-wheel trailer 999 carrying a Parsons transformer on 12 September 1967.

**Above** Sea-going vessels like barges have obviously also to be utilized for any loads being imported into the country. The Tom Llewellyn photograph taken in July 1980 shows a Belgian column coming ashore at the Thames estuary. The move was the first joint venture of the company Mammoet-Econofreight which was set up at that time to replace the Mammoet-owned Magnaload operations. The Volvo F89 tractor unit is still currently in use by Econofreight.

**Below** The ability to reconstruct your load-carrying trailers to meet the changing demands of traffic was to revolutionize the heavier end of abnormal traffic movements. Seen on 12 June 1986 at Hawker Siddeley, Walthamstow, Dereck Dawson is at the wheel of A516 HVN which is coupled to a four-deck-four trailer which includes a specially-constructed thin deck designed by Keith Johnson. This ensured that the running height of the 90 ton transformer was kept to a minimum. Bob Bridges the transport manager of Hawker Siddeley is observing the departure of the outfit *en route* to Vauxhall Motors at Luton.

**Above** Were it not for the modular concept of trailer building, it is doubtful whether record-breaking loads like this could be moved in one piece, the method that construction engineers prefer. Dave Gardner, Shell's Stanlow photographer, was swung 75 ft up in a hoist to capture this regenerator in proper perspective as it negotiated the turn from the M53 slip road on to the A5117 road on Sunday 14 December 1986. All-up travelling weight was recorded as 1,200 tonnes whilst Econofreight utilized 416 Nicolas wheels in 26 rows of axles in a configuration known as four file wide. Movement for the 5½ miles between Ellesmere Port and Stanlow at less than an average 1 mph was done by Peter Clemmett in the Tractomas headed up by two Mark 2 Contractors.

**Below** There are always going to be loads that need something different to haul them and in the Southampton area miles of special Pirelli cable are hauled regularly on this strange looking bobbin carrier. Tony Kimber's service van heads up the ex-Pickfords 240 ton Scammell Contractor whilst the Detroit powered Scammell Samson is out of sight pushing at the rear. Seen crossing the subway on Milbrooke Road, Southampton, the cable carrier hauls its specially-made produce between the Pirelli premises at Eastleigh and Southampton docks.

# 5. Wheels on wheels

To most of us the motor car is a necessity, to some it may still be considered a luxury, but to all who have the fortune of the use of one, the motor car is a form of independence, offering the sheer freedom of being able to go in the direction and at the speed you desire. No one can argue with the general supposition that the car is built to be driven on the road. To place it immediately on the back of another large motor vehicle piggy-back style as soon as it is built for its journey to distant parts seems stranger than fiction. But modern-day car transportation is very big business, involving the movement of millions of vehicles each year on purpose-built lorries.

Until the general concept of car transporters was imported from the United States after the Second World War, the 'plater' ruled. His name was derived from the incongruous temporary number plates affixed to a new vehicle by oversized rubber bands. The plater could be seen anywhere between Land's End and John O'Groats as the cars made their way outwards at varying rates of knots from their base in the car maker's triangle. By and large the plater lived at or very close to places like Dagenham, Oxford, Birmingham, Coventry or Luton, for the vast majority of our road vehicles were being produced out of this portion of England.

It should be understood that at this time all new vehicles were sold by the manufacturer to their respective dealers as 'ex works'. In other words the dealer was responsible for the car once it was built and it was his problem to get it from the factory once it had left the production line. Many of course dispatched their own staff to go and collect the new vehicles but the entrepreneurs spawned in the early era of the mass-produced motor car found that by setting up in business as delivery agents, they could offer those far-flung dealers a very worthwhile service. A lot endeavoured to follow, although few were able to match the service that was offered by a man called Henry.

William Morris, who was later to become Lord Nuffield, had struck up a friendship with Captain B. J. Henry during the First World War, and it was with Morris's encouragement that Henry founded the first specialized vehicle delivery service working out of the Morris factory at Cowley near Oxford. Just as Messrs Rolls and Royce were the cream of the motor car industry, so Henry was the cream of the vehicle deliverers. Staff were screened rigorously prior to being employed, with a stiff driving test being one of the things which had to be passed before any prospective candidate could be taken on. Henry's firm felt that delivering a new car by road required an entirely different driving technique, with car appreciation and sympathy being of the utmost importance. Henry's were later to claim in their publicity material of the 1950s that they delivered ¼ million vehicles over a distance of 26 million miles without a single complaint. B. J. Henry had the full time staff to be able to run convoys to the docks and when these were organized, motor cycle outriders were utilized to keep the convoy together and rule out difficulties with stragglers. It was not unknown to see in excess of 50 brand new vehicles travelling nose to tail, although with numbers like this in the offing the railways were soon to take a strong interest in the possibility of delivery.

Strangely it wasn't British Rail who was to take the lead, or more correctly speaking any of the various regional railways that were currently operating, but once again entrepreneurs. A. Kunzler and A. H. Moser got together to form Machinery and Technical Transport who in 1926 had pioneered the export of cars in a completely unpacked condition by rail to Europe. Prior to this cars had either been exported as a large package or in a form known as CKD — completely knocked down — to be reassembled later anywhere on the globe. Machinery and Technical Transport had quite an influence on the movement of the motor car, and it was interesting to note that in 1937 the French Railways introduced special ferry wagons with end doors for car movements which were built to Machinery's own special requirements. The Second World War was to bring about a complete diversification of this company's operations, so to promote the new image the lengthy old title was dropped and MAT Transport Ltd was formed. Immediately after the war, MAT was organizing special trains carrying cars via Dieppe and Calais, but back at home the number of platers were steadily on the increase.

Up until the middle 1960s, there were two completely different types of trade plate: the 'general' plate had white letters on a red background and a small oblong on the top of the plate giving the details of the holder; the 'limited' trade plate had red letters on a white background and the details of its holder were contained in a triangle shape at the top of the plate. The general plate, as its name suggests, could be used for virtually anything, so long as the purpose was loosely connected with the motor trade, and did permit certain car transporters to use them legally. The limited trade plate in contrast, which cost only £5 for a year, had a more restricted use, although delivery of individual brand new cars was of course one of the things that could be done with them. To remind police officers of the gulf between these two different types of trade plate a little saying was passed by training instructors: 'White on red, go ahead; red on white, stop on sight.'

B. J. Henry was undoubtedly one of the leaders in trade plate delivery of separate cars, but to the firm's great credit it did not remain complacent and in fact became one of the leaders in adopting the awe-inspiring double deck car transporter. In 1949 a fleet of six new four-car transporters took to the road and although in the main they were carrying 'Nuffield Exports To The World' running between Cowley and the London docks, the seed of national car transporter delivery service was sown.

Henry's new transporters were nothing if not distinctive. A three or four-axled artic found Morris Commercial tractors being adopted as the prime mover. The Brockhouse semi-trailer had a two-tier construction, although, with the top deck fixed in position, loading/unloading was a somewhat precarious procedure. The tractor unit was first unhitched, moved out of the way and the landing legs of the semi-trailer wound down so that the front of the trailer virtually begged for attention. Two cars were then driven up ramps over the front of the trailer and on to the top deck. By winding the landing legs back down with the exertion of considerably more physical effort, the semi-trailer stood itself up and allowed the tractor unit to hitch up once more. The two cars for the lower deck were driven on via the back of the trailer in conventional fashion and after securing the vehicles in position the transporter was ready for the road.

The fixed double deck car transporter is now considered archaic in its conception, although varying forms were still used by different operators until well into the 1960s. The alternative to unhitching the tractor was to use excessively long ramps strengthend by scissored supports so that the cars could be driven, rather slowly, straight up on to the top deck. Handling of these ramps was also heavy work and it took a brave man to drive this incline for many was the tale of the ramps slipping to leave cars scrambling up or down to safety.

One interesting alternative method of loading the top fixed deck was practised by one go-ahead northern operator who ran one of these outfits for quite a while, although generally it ran in close company with a conventional outfit with a movable top deck. The method used to load the static deck transporter was simply to load up the other outfit's top deck in the normal manner, jack knife the two artics to allow them to close together and then drive the cars from one top deck to the other 12 ft off the ground without so much as a shudder.

Big competitors of Morris Cars were of course Austin Motors from Birmingham, and they were in fact operating their own distinctive double-deckers as early as 1948. The car transporter thus became a more regular sight, especially around the Metropolis *en route* to the London docks. They still turned the eye not only of followers of cars and transport, but also of the general public who were mildly buffeted by the air as they swished past or as they seemed to defy the laws of physics by leaning over to take the bends.

One observer who studied these new car transporters more closely than most was William E. Herbert, the chief designer from Carrimore Six Wheelers of Finchley. Herbert had the foresight to identify that the car transporter was an exciting new project, provided he could invent a system which would allow the top deck to go up and down and so dispense with the awful loading nightmare. Herbert worked closely with chief draughtsman A. E. Line and draughtsman Alan Cooper, and their brilliant swinging link concept was the basis of an outfit that was to become market leader for nearly 15 years and make the name Carrimore synonymous with car transportation.

The original two Mark 1 Carrimores were built for Hartwells of Oxford and had a capacity of four cars, similar to the transporters then in use. However, in extending the top deck, so that when it was in the raised position the deck went over the cab of the tractor unit, the capacity of the Mark 2 Carrimore was for five vehicles of most sizes.

The idea of selling new cars with virtually no mileage on the clock soon appealed to the trade outlets round the country with the bigger garage chains either investing in their own transporters or having hauliers' vehicles painted in their contract colours. The Carrimore Mark 2 became the standard transporter to have, although the Finchley factory saw some strange people come and collect their new outfits.

Prior to the arrival of the car transporter, some up-market car dealers had always used a driver complete with fine uniform, peaked cap, gauntlets and boots to deliver their new vehicles to the customer and thus present a very fine image. It was thus two such attired drivers who came to the London factory one day to take over the machine that would allow them to deliver four or five vehicles at the same time. Obviously more used to chauffeuring the individual limousine, neither driver felt that looking out for low bridges should be of any concern, but later the same day both transporters were to be damaged as their respective new drivers struck the superstructure of two different rather low railway bridges.

Even running empty the Carrimore's ram stuck out skywards like two prominent fingers. Originally fitted with Edbro tipper rams to lift the upper deck, drivers had to ensure they pressurized these rams prior to unloading so that the descent of the top deck was done in an orderly, controlled fashion. It was not a rare occasion that due to either human or hydraulic pressure failure in operating the upper deck saw it descend at a frightening rate of knots, the shock of which would take a year or two off the operator's life.

Even with these obvious operational drawbacks the Carrimore order book was overflowing and a delivery wait of two years was not unusual. Strangely the competition in such a buoyant market was rather fragmented and although Brockhouse were early pioneers, they did not sustain this with good market share. Taskers of Andover produced their own distinctive car carrier using a Burtonwood tail lift to carry individual cars up to the two fixed decks. Loading time was always going to be slower than the Carrimore, but if you had to load vehicles by pushing them on because their engines wouldn't start for some reason, the tail lift could always be flexed in a favourable angular direction so that the non-runners could be made to free-wheel onboard.

One other major difference between the Carrimore and Tasker outfits was that the Carrimore standardized on a fixed coupling and separation of the tractor/semi-trailer was rather an old fashioned workshop job. Taskers used a variation of the Scammell type of automatic coupling which thus allowed for brisk separation of the semi-trailer if needed. However, in their favour Carrimores had long advocated the use of the retractable turntable which meant that when the artic turned a corner, the gap between the back of the driver's cab and the semi-trailer headboard was increased to prevent any fouling.

The car transporter was obviously a big asset to the road transport industry although John Thompson recalled that not everyone appreciated the sight of this newfangled lorry. At the time John was driving SJR 100, the sole car transporter of the W. A. Glendenning fleet running out of Island Garage, Shotley Bridge in north-west Durham. It being one of the few car carriers in the area, John was asked to collect a new Rolls-Royce for a north-east dealer, although the greeting he received when he went to the factory was not particularly cordial.

'It's not going on that thing,' the incensed RR man said as John was trying to arrange for the loading of his cargo. 'Its got a wheel on each corner, they are made to be driven on the road and that's what we built them for,' was the argument put forward, and even diplomatic John couldn't contest this line of reasoning, so the car in question was eventually driven to the dealer up country by road.

The quantity of car transporters on the road in the late 1950s may have been on the increase but they were still in small enough numbers to be more like a tightly-knit fraternity greeting each other with light flashing and arm waving, even though as individual drivers they may not have known each other. Written on the side of the transporters were evocative sayings like 'Nuffield Exports To The World', 'More Rootes Cars For Ray Powell', 'Car

Transporters To The North East', 'Still More Vauxhalls & Bedfords For SMT', 'Jaguar World Wide Exports Delivered On Guy', 'More Minxes For Minories', and 'Cars Transported By Road Scotland-England'.

The car transporter operators of this era fell into three distinct types. The small independents were spread thinly round the country with people like Glendennings of Shotley Bridge, Reliability Car Collection of Bradford, A. & C. McClennan of Perth, Overland Transporters of Carlisle, Robson & Everard of Hexham, A. & D. Frazer of Glasgow and John K. Gordon of Aberdeen.

The transporters operated either by the car manufacturers or dealers were normally identified by the use of general trade plates on their vehicles, with Austin Motors being one of this type of operator who developed their fleet into quite some numbers. Other names in this bracket were Smarts of Newcastle, Melvins Motors of Glasgow, Marshall Sea Brothers of Taunton and Bristol Street Motors of Birmingham.

However, the biggest operators of all car transporters were the specialists like Autocar's of Alvechurch, Furness & Parker of Coventry, Toleman's of Dagenham, Canley Car Delivery of Kenilworth and B. J. Henry of Oxford, although the leaders of the pack were indoubtedly the aptly named Progressive Deliveries who were based at Tile Hill near Coventry. Progressives had a pleasing blue-based livery, but the main distinctive part about their fleet was that they standardized on Leyland Comets rather than the lightweight BMC, Commer and Thames Traders favoured by the opposition.

Another well-remembered operator had a black and white colour scheme with the letters BTC in prominent size. This stood for Barnett Transport Company of Birmingham although confusion in its meaning did allow for some deliveries that should never really have taken place.

The story is told of one convoy of BTC vehicles going to the London docks when they were being picketed by strikers over one matter or another. The only goods vehicles the striking dockers would allow through the picket line were those being operated by the nationalized concerns, which in essence meant British Road Services. When this was explained to the leading BTC driver quick as a flash he retorted 'Well that means us as well.' The pickets didn't understand what he meant until the driver explained that BTC did in fact stand for British Transport Commision and was obviously in the same category as BRS vehicles but just a different colour. This explanation may have been a little white lie, but the fib opened the gates and the convoy was allowed in to unload the vehicles.

It was not until the early 1960s that the wagon and drag made any impression on the predominance of articulated car transporters. Autocar's had run a converted four-wheeled Leyland Steer and drag — SJY 545 — that had started life in the colours of the Plymouth Transport Co, but like the AEC Mercury based outfit — WKV 183 — of Masterways of Coventry, it was rather a one off. The drawbar outfit did allow for 9 cars to be carried but its first design was in essence a duplication of identical superstructures both on the wagon and trailer. This meant the trailer had to be unhitched before the wagon was loaded and as well as being a slow process, the combination was both heavy and rather expensive to produce.

But what was to happen during the 1960s was to turn the industry on its head and catapult car transportation into the realms of very big business, with one man in particular exerting a major influence towards higher efficiency through an ability to carry more and more vehicles as fee-earning payload.

Alastair Carter was an engineer by profession and during the 1950s he was employed by Abelson's at Sheldon in the design and construction of dumper bodies. As a slight diversion he was asked to repair a short-coupled car carrying drawbar trailer for Major Lea, the owner of Avon Car Deliveries. The outfit was too weak to carry the Land-Rovers it was intended to, so Alastair designed and built a light alloy sloper on an Albion chassis. As the term suggests, this vehicle had a fixed sloping deck but was still capable of carrying three vehicles with ease.

Alastair went on to build another three or four similar vehicles and they were quite popular around that time, but Abelson's were not really interested in car carriers and called a stop to the practice. Alastair on the other hand saw massive prospects and taking the plunge he set up on his own at Tamworth. The slopers may have been fairly easy to construct and coupled to a small trailer they could in fact carry five vehicles, but Alastair knew that if he was to make any impact on the virtual Carrimore monopoly then he must think big, but also think different.

In offering the electric lift mechanism rather than the hydraulic rams of the Finchley builder, prospective customers for car-carrying outfits could now consider the Carter as a direct alternative. The electric motor working through a screw deck mechanism could not fail in the frightening way that hydraulics were known to, and making the rear two threads of a coarser pitch meant that, if desired, the deck was angled in a suitable manner as it lowered itself down.

The electric/threaded screw lift mechanism was incorporated into the Carter Carveyor, this being the title given to Alastair's wagon and drag which was produced in direct competition to the newly-produced, similarly-configured Carrimore. Both outfits had the same basic loading pattern in that the top deck of the trailer was loaded by driving vehicles through the lower deck of the trailer on to the drawing vehicle. In the case of the Carter, the electric lift raised the vehicles to the upper deck one at a time although the Carrimore's upper deck lowered via a pair of hydraulic rams and hinged to give a reasonable slope from a point just behind the top of the driving cab. Once on the upper deck of the drawing vehicle, the cars were reversed across inter-linking ramping on to the top deck of the trailer.

Whether you used Carter or Carrimore super structure and drawbar trailer, the natural choice of drawing vehicle saw a Leyland predominance because the early 1960s were days when the Super Comet reigned supreme. The Leyland 400 engine mated to the Albion-built, six-speed gearbox and Eaton two-speed axle gave the wagon and drag a performance that would regularly see 60 mph on the speedometer. Even fitted with full air brakes it was still a handful to stop, and on basic steel suspension with a full load it would sway and lean like a romantic sailing clipper; but the Super Comet was something rather special.

The obvious difference in the Carter and Carrimore Leylands was that with a sprinkling of fashionable, smaller models, the Carter could carry 11 cars compared to a maximum of only nine on the Carrimore. The simple reason for that was that the Carter was about 10 ft longer than the Carrimore, so naturally it had the potential to carry the two more vehicles.

An apparent abuse of the length regulations brought the wrath of several Police Forces down against the Carveyor operators. All were to be exonerated as Alastair proved his sharpness in reading the finer points of the law as he successfully argued that detachable extensions should not be considered as part of the vehicle. It was to take a change in the law in 1965 to shake this reasoning, but even before that Alastair went one better with his half cabs which would in fact carry 12 cars when fully loaded.

Based on Leyland Leopard and AEC Reliance bus chassis with underfloor engines these new Carter outfits incorporated some of Alastair's dumper know-how, for using that type of cab he realized he could get a Mini or Hillman Imp alongside the driver and squeeze yet another fee-earning vehicle on board.

BTC ran about six of the big half cabs and driver Albert Ellis reckoned it was the best motor he had for sheer power and smoothness. He did not like the loading pattern, for the car alongside him created quite a blind spot to the nearside. Albert recalled that with only inches to spare at either side of the wheel, you could certainly rap your knuckles if your hand slipped whilst manoeuvring in a tight spot.

Whilst the half cab's were undoubtedly of great engineering brilliance, the ironical part about them was that as the drivers were in dispute with BTC over payment of higher rates for their use, the unions dictated that only 9 or 10 vehicles should be carried on the transporter. In the car-carrying business the strength of union power was something not to be under estimated.

There were regular battles in the middle 1960s, some of which touched on the fight to save the jobs of the thousands of trade plate drivers. The efficiency of the car transporter, which after 1965 could then carry up to 7 cars on an artic due to longer overall length rules, meant that the days of the massive use of platers were numbered. It was only natural that there was a great deal of bitterness as car transporters were now being developed to carry new truck and bus chassis — the platers domain for years — and even general cargo.

The concept of a car transporter hauling differing types of payload from wheeled vehicles is a natural progression of thought because, like other highly specialized vehicles, the empty running of some transporters can be as high as 50 per cent of the actual road mileage.

Early advocates of this argument were Hoynor of Braintree in Essex who entered the car transporter market in about 1965. The clean simple lines of their Mark 2 semi-trailer soon found favour, and many are still in regular use today. Hoynor — set up by Mr Hoy and Mr Norton — were well-known for their tipping trailers, but prided themselves on an ability to present good solutions to difficult transport problems. Such was their expertise that they modified their Mark 2 into the Mark 3 Transloader, the significance in the later model being that the top deck lowered to a totally flat position and thus allowed space to carry general cargo on top of the car deck frames.

With only three axles, the Hoynor-based artic was obviously limited to 24 tons gross, although Ken Glendenning worked closely with Alan Cooper of Carrimore to produce a similar dual-purpose outfit capable of running at the then maximum of 32 tons train weight. Glendenning's first CVC — cars, vans, cargo — took to the road in 1972 and even with its substantial superstructure could carry 18 tons of payload. Steel plate from Consett Iron Company was a natural south-bound load, and, as the CVC immediately proved its viability, six more similar trailers were ordered.

Whilst this dual-purpose role was ideal for general hauliers like Glendenning, the car transporter specialists felt it was more of an erosion of standards and a confrontation with the unions arose. Glendennings had to decide whether their trailers were car transporters or cargo carriers; they had to be one or the other, not both, so the dual role was called to an end.

Further relaxation of the length limits allowing artics to run up to 15 m did not really increase their capacity; the trend with popular cars saw their individual sizes grow in length as the likes of the Mini and Hillman Imp started to lose in popularity in favour of cars similar to the Ford Escort. So it was at this point that the engineering of car transporters grew more important in line with major changes going on in the car moving industry.

Following a trend set originally by the importing car manufacturers, with Nissan being the only major dissenter, car transporter operators were now winning contracts to deliver cars to specific areas of the country. This practice followed a change in the fine print in that a vehicle was now no longer sold 'ex works', but a delivery charge was incorporated as one of the mandatory extras to each new car as the manufacturer/importer took over the responsibility of delivering his new vehicles to the dealer's premises. So instead of servicing individual dealers or chains of garages, the transporter operator was now working direct for the vehicle manufacturer or his UK importer.

In effect this change meant that the small operator with only one or two outfits who delivered to his local outlets, or even the garages who collected vehicles on their own transporters, were virtually wiped out of transportation or if not severely limited in the work they could do.

Nissan went against the grain by setting up their own transporter business under the banner of Car Removal Ltd, and although they ran a small number of transporters themselves, they tended to employ the smaller operator for their nation-wide deliveries.

This instance apart, the trend was for the big specialist operator to get bigger through mergers or buy-outs of smaller operations to take over their slice of the contracted market share. Many famous names were to soon disappear including the pioneer of them all, B. J. Henry. They were taken over by Autocar of Birmingham in 1962, although the trading name was retained until 1972. Dealers Deliveries, who in turn had taken over the interests of MVT, Vehicle Clearances, LB Convoys, Ellesmere Deliveries and others, were themselves taken over by Autocar. This Birmingham operator grew to be one of the biggest, with the take-over of Dependable Deliveries, but in 1980 this trading name was dropped as unfortunately whenever there was the slighest hiccup with a delivery, the haulier was, nicknamed Undependable or Diabolical.

British Road Services were also very strong in the car transporter field and in 1964 they acquired Furness & Parker of Coventry. In 1974 Lathams Transport Ltd were absorbed for their substantial import contracts and a year later Autoclearances Ltd were also acquired.

It was not only the established names who grew in size but also the diverse habitats of Kirriemuir in Fife and Yeovil, Somerset, were to spawn the operations of Richard Lawson and Roger Bastable. It was to be the latter, R. K. Bastable Ltd, trading under the name of Abbey Hill, who were to make the biggest in-roads towards the market leaders of Tolemans Delivery Services. From their original base at Dagenham, the family-owned group of Tolemans grew to become arguably the leader in the car-carrying field, with a fleet size in excess of 300 transporters working nation-wide following the absorption of the interests of firms like James Delivery Service, BTC, A. & C. McClennan and previous business front runners, Progressives.

This trend towards excessively large fleets meant a keen competition in the tendering for vehicle contracts and although some of these contracts only lasted two or three years, the standing charges alone for two or three hundred vehicles meant there was immense pressure on the operators to win these contracts just to keep the transporters at work.

The accountants in the business thus expected more from their counterpart engineers with a view to increasing the basic payload of seven vehicles on an artic and eight on a drawbar outfit. With the law tightly controlling both the overall length and width of an outfit, best use had thus to be made of the available space inside these constraints. There was no limit as to the height of an outfit and triple-deck artics were soon to appear. These were only marginally successful as damage, particularly from low overhead trees, could be counterproductive, even though two more cars could be carried. The answer, however, to more productivity was simple if perhaps more exacting, as the realization was made that the overall length of a vehicle could be reduced if it was stacked on the transporter at an angle.

The vogue of fitting small collapsible ramps on to the main internal decks of a car transporter soon caught on. Their one obvious disadvantage was that manoeuvring up these acute inclines, even for the very short distance involved, could be very taxing both on the driver and on the vehicle's transmission. Hoynor once again came to prominence, as they adopted sophisticated hydraulics into their trailers so that the vehicles were ramped up or down after they had been driven on to the transporter, thus saving a great deal in driver and transmission wear.

Hoynor themselves had undergone a major transition because in 1969 the receiver had been called in as hard times affected the business. It was to be three ex-employees — John Lambert, William Perdeaux and Arthur Vale — who were to buy the trading name and patents, so ensuring the continuance of the British car transporter manufacturer as imports, especially from Lohr, became dominant. The famous Carrimores had been bought by the York Group, whilst Alastair Carter sold out to Crane Fruehauf in 1973, although neither of these two massive trailer builders continued to have a major influence on the transporter market. Carrimore/York continued in production until the middle of the 1980s with the building being transferred first from Finchley to Harelaw in County Durham and then to Northallerton in North Yorkshire. Municipal Trailers of Preston came on to the market place until the 1980s with some popular wagon and drags, but it was to be the Hoynor Mark 7 semi-trailer that was to stand the test of time from its introduction in 1971.

The Mark 7 is still in vast use today, later models having air suspension and some of these trailers modified to carry an eighth car slung hammock-style in the small space between the upper and lower decks. Named the 'Cavalier Ramp' after the Vauxhall it was first designed to carry, this innovation opened the floodgates for engineering flair. The 1980s were awash with complicated variations into ramping, stacking and even triple-decking came back into popularity as the search for the perfect system to carry more cars, more of the time was fuelled by the need to win the major movement contracts.

*Motor-cycle patrols are a B. J. Henry Ltd. innovation. Acting much in the same way as Army despatch riders, they help the convoy leaders to control and co-ordinate journeys*

*In 25 years B. J. Henry Ltd. have satisfactorily delivered more than 750,000 vehicles*

## THE B. J. HENRY LTD. SERVICE

**Our Chauffeur Service . . . .**

During the Coronation we were pleased to be able to assist several distinguished overseas visitors by placing uniformed chauffeurs at their disposal throughout their stay in Great Britain.

Chauffeurs can be hired for a few hours, or by the day, week or month, for weddings, theatres, race meetings or touring holidays, at very reasonable charges. We shall be pleased to quote rates if you will let us know your requirements.

*B. J. Henry Ltd. were the first delivery agents to offer Transporter facilities. These vehicles are now a familiar sight in dockland areas*

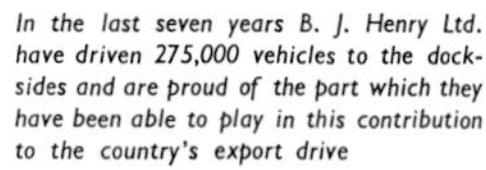

*In the last seven years B. J. Henry Ltd. have driven 275,000 vehicles to the docksides and are proud of the part which they have been able to play in this contribution to the country's export drive*

**B. J. HENRY LTD. · VEHICLE DELIVERY SPECIALISTS**

**c/o MORRIS MOTORS LTD. · COWLEY · OXFORD** **Telephone : Oxford 77004**

*(Left.) The coupling mechanism of B. J. Henry's new transporter to the Morris-Commercial Diesel-engined prime mover.*

*(Right.) New Morris cars ascending the ramp to the top deck of one of B. J. Henry's new car transporters.*

*Of interest to every Distributor and Dealer . .*

PIONEERS in the car delivery business, B. J. Henry Limited have a reputation which is your guarantee of complete satisfaction. We are proud to announce that once again we are leading the way with the introduction of a fleet of six new four-car transporters.

On the B. J. Henry transporters, once the car has left the factory it does not run another mile until it is in the customer's possession.

Here, indeed, is a valuable sales point. All car owners like to have " nothing on the clock " when taking delivery. B. J. Henry Limited will see to it that *your* cars are delivered in absolutely mint condition, to your entire satisfaction and that of your customer. We believe this method of car delivery to be of interest to every Distributor and Dealer, and we shall be pleased to send a representative to discuss this matter in full detail at your convenience.

*A Morris Minor enters the lower deck of the car transporter.*

**Above** Captain B.J. Henry, encouraged by Lord Nuffield, set up the first specialized vehicle delivery service in 1919. His employees initially worked out of the Morris factory at Cowley and delivered the individual cars by road fitted with limited trade plates. Their publicity material illustrates the professional attitude adopted by this company who were later to be absorbed into Western Motor Holdings.

**Left** B.J. Henry may have built their company up using trade plate drivers, but they quickly appreciated the advantages of offering vehicle delivery with virtually 'nothing on the clock'. Their first transporters, however, now seem rather antiquated in the extreme for they even required the semi-trailer to be unhitched before the top deck could be loaded.

**Above** In contrast to the fixed deck transporters, the swinging link concept of Carrimore's first Mark 1 was the key to a transporter far in advance of any others then on offer. Designed by William E. Herbert, the outfit is pictured outside the Swan & Pyramids public house, North Finchley which was known to all at the factory as Carrimore's annex.

**Above right** This Brockhouse transporter of 1956 utilized a similar type of tipper ram to raise and lower the upper deck combined with a set of roller guides to hold the moving deck in position. Even though it did not have the rams protruding skywards Carrimore style, the make was never as popular as the Finchley outfit. The Ford Thames is carrying three four door Ford Prefects and one two-door Ford Anglia.

**Right** Austin Motors were one of the few vehicle manufacturers who also ran their own transporters, mainly to carry vehicles destined for export. Their first transporters were run as early as 1948, although this Austin photograph illustrates an outfit dating from 1956. The managing director of Austin around that time was Mr L.P. Lord who had the factory's own transporters made in the plant after seeing similar machines at work on a visit to America.

**Left and below left** SJR 100 was north-west Durham's first home-based car transporter, bought by Glendennings because of the long waiting-list for Carrimore outfits. The fixed-deck Taskers semi-trailer was fitted with a Burtonwood tail lift meaning that vehicles had to be loaded/unloaded on an individual basis. John Thompson was the outfit's first regular driver, seen here unloading Vauxhall Victors and Bedford CA vans in Front Street, Consett.

**Below** The Autocar Group with their head office at Wythall, Birmingham, are now one of the big concerns in modern-day car transportation. They trace their history back to 1948 when they started out with individual trade plate deliveries and soon expanded into transporters. This line up of Carrimore-based outfits carrying Austins, seen in about 1956, includes two bonneted Austin Loadstar tractive units fitted with the Perkins engine.

**Above and right** There are always going to be cars built that cannot be carried using conventional transporters. Graham Adams Ltd took responsibility for the delivery of Donald Campbell's *Bluebird* to the Utah salt flats in 1959. The Seddon SD4 tractor unit was coupled to a 35 ft platform Carrimore semi-trailer which needed ramps 40 ft long for unloading. All-up payload including *Bluebird* and assorted equipment was about 10 tons, which was road-hauled 2,500 miles after disembarkation at New York.

**Right** The sloper is and always has been a simple, efficient way of carrying up to three vehicles that can be loaded/unloaded quickly on a vehicle built at minimum cost. It was also the first type of transporter to be built by Alastair Carter when he was employed at Abelsons of Sheldon as an aside to his normal dumper body construction.

When hauling a close-coupled drawbar trailer, the sloper was capable of carrying five vehicles and thus could be directly compared to the conventional articulated transporter. Agricultural tractors have always been a regular cargo, the two alternative methods of transporting them being shown here. Mortons of Coventry used to specialize in carrying tractors across their semi-trailers, a practice eventually curtailed when restrictions were placed on the ever-increasing width of these outfits.

**Right and below right** The wagon and drag outfit was the obvious way towards greater carrying capacity. The first Carrimores of this type sported a duplication of the lifting deck superstructure and were thus both heavy and expensive. The design also necessitated the trailer being unhitched prior to loading/unloading of the drawing vehicle. The outfit on show is WKV 183, an AEC Mercury operated by Masterways of Coventry, pictured outside the Carrimore annex on loading trials, with the front upper deck supporting two Humber Hawks.

**Below** The subsequent Carrimore production on the drawbar outfit was far more popular, since the fixed decks on the drawbar trailer meant that the upper deck was loaded by reversing vehicles from the upper deck of the drawing vehicle across small bridging plates. The Glendennings outfit is unloading in Newcastle about June 1964, with Vauxhall Vivas, one Victor and a Victor VX 4/90. Robert Tuck was to be this outfit's regular trailer attendant for the first 18 months of its life.

**Left** The Carter alternative to the similar Carrimore outfit was known as the Carveyor. With a liberal mix of the popular Mini, eleven vehicles could be carried, including two long Austin Cambridges, as opposed to the maximum of nine on a Carrimore. BTC ran a number of these Super Comet outfits, registered 281 KOG, 242 HNP, 695 JVP, 745 HNP, 985 JVP.

**Below left and bottom** The half cabs were undoubtedly the biggest head-turners the industry had ever seen. Even without the need to stack the cars on ramps, up to 12 vehicles could be carried. Underfloor-engined bus chassis had to be used to allow the foremost vehicle room. The one advantage the McLennan outfit had was that in hauling a small trailer it did not need to carry a trailer man. It is carrying Imps, Minxes, a Super Minx, a Husky and Sunbeam Rapier, all sourced from the Rootes Group of manufacturers.

**Opposite page** Following their outstanding success in rallying, the Mini Cooper S was raced all over Europe. This transporter was specially built in the early '60s by Carrimores for the Cooper organization who wished to carry these cars to meetings on the Continent. The large compartment on the lower deck was to carry engines and other spare parts. The price of the petrol then on sale equates to about 22p a gallon.

ELMBRIDGE 3346-9167
The COOPER
CAR COMPANY LIMITED
SURBITON ENGLAND
BMC
MINI-COOPERS
MINI-COOPERS
AUSTIN
552 PB

COOPER
SURBITON ENGLAND
BP
SUPER PLUS
BP
SUPER
BP
REGULAR
REGULAR
BP
5689 PE

**Left** With the legislators restricting the Carter interpretation of wagon and trailer outfits, Alastair turned his attention to the articulated market. This Autocar example was one of the later 510 15 metre outfits. The typical Carter angular framework was extremely light, the tubular members being joined up with triangular gusset plates. Also of note was the Carter underslung trailer suspension which allowed such a low loading height.

**Right and background photograph** Hoynor of Braintree, Essex came into the car transporter market during the 1960s, many versions of their simply-built Mark two still being in use today. The use of conventional suspension and tyres on the semi-trailer axle meant loading height was higher than the opposition but the straight run on to the upper deck allowed for bus chassis movement if required.

**Right** Hoynor also constructed this purpose-built chassis carrier in 1970 although restrictions in lower deck inner width were always going to be a problem. Dealers Deliveries were one of the few operators who favoured the stronger Foden tractive unit. They also ran a number of half-cab Fodens on transporter work. Dealers were later to be absorbed into the Autocar Group.

**This page** Built at Harelaw, County Durham, these Carrimore outfits demonstrated the flair in design work needed in the car transporter business. The rocking of the centre part of the deck allowed for up to four commercial vehicles to be carried but mathematics will show that the all-up outfit was particularly heavy. Restrictive union practices meant that these outfits — one built for Tolemans, the other for Silcocks — never were an operational success.

**Right** Not perhaps in the same class for sheer numbers but still ingenious, this Peter Lee photograph taken in South Wales illustrates an innovative way of piggy-backing a rigid goods vehicle. As a matter of interest the tipper body of the Scania 86 was carrying a small crawler machine.

**Right and below** As a concept the CVC — Cars, Vans, Cargo — was brilliant in that it could cut down dramatically on the unladen running of a transporter by allowing it to carry general cargo when wheeled vehicles were not available. Alan Cooper of Carrimore and Ken Glendenning conceived this idea which in appearance was based on a standard Mark seven transporter. Eight of these were made for Glendennings, the last six being on smaller 8.25 × 15 twin tyres. The CVC's use was eventually stopped following overtures made by the car transporter drivers' union.

**Above** The triple decker was an obvious step towards greater capacity, this Carrimore version being based on the lines of their Mark Nine double-deck semi-trailer. Although the engineering was quite complicated, it was to be the physical running height of the outfit that was to prove its biggest restriction. The cargo being carried is left-hand-drive Morris 1100 saloons.

**Left** Whilst overhanging trees and branches are a continual headache to transporter drivers, the punishment of low bridges can be more severe. Rather than being most upset, the Saab dealer very close to where this saloon was due to be delivered insisted that the incident be recorded for posterity. No one could argue with him when he said it clearly portrayed how strong the Saab roof was if it could hold the car simply wedged in this position!

**Above** Rolls-Royce are probably one of the few manufacturers who are not over concerned in transporter capacity, which may be connected to the fact that their most costly production car is the Phantom VI which has a price tag of £207,332. The 1979 Clydesdale shown in this Rolls-Royce photograph is about to leave Crewe for the Mulliner Park Ward division in London. The two vehicles heavily sheeted are partially completed Corniche Convertibles *en route* for completion.

**Below** Trading under the name of Car Removal Ltd, Nissan UK are one of the few current manufacturers/importers who run their own transporter fleet. They are also probably the only concern to undertake all deliveries mainly by using subcontracted hauliers. This Dick Shepherd photograph shows a Teesport-based DAF 2800 carrying a superstructure built by Municipal Trailers Ltd of Preston. The 2800 was one of the most powerful transporters on the road at a time when the wagon and drag outfits were limited to 30 mph on roads other than motorways.

**Above and left** The Hoynor Mark 7 has proved to be a versatile transporter for its Braintree manufacturer. With modification, the Cavalier ramp was devised to raise its general capacity to eight fairly large saloons. The eighth car rests in a hammock which is swung between the two normal decks.

**Left** This Car Transport photograph shows a slightly smaller but no less significant ramp insertion allowing for an increase in capacity. The Leyland Roadtrain tractor unit was one of 18 new units leased to work out of the Austin Longbridge plant. It is powered by the Rolls-Royce 265 engine and fitted with the short Jennings sleeper cab conversion.

**Above** The Toleman Group have long been strong advocates of the Lohr transporter made in France, feeling that its lightweight build on an Iveco chassis is the only legal way of carrying nine exceptionally heavy saloons. The stacking method which is currently the vogue adopted in loading transporters is clearly shown. The latest Lohr transporters were to incorporate screw thread mechanisms of a similar design to those used by Alastair Carter on his Carveyor, 25 years earlier.

**Below** Hoynor have taken over the mantle of leading British transporter manufacturer. They relish in new design work with 'one-offs' to meet a customer's special requirements, although in this type of wagon and trailer outfit, they feel the trend for more capacity has gone. A tri-axle trailer is adopted to give greater stability and minimize distortion or cracking in the trailer superstructure.

# Postscript

Car transportation, if anything, epitomizes the current trends in carrying cargo as the ever competitive market place screams out for more efficiency. Vehicles are being built now that can carry more payload at faster speeds, yet still with the awareness for better fuel consumption. The key in these transitions ever onward has always to be the figure behind the wheel, normally a servant to the employer, sometimes an owner/driver but always someone who simply wants to do a good day's work.

In looking at the changes in the lorry and how it carries cargo, I do not think we should ever forget its driver and the adaptations he is expected to absorb in this changing world. To describe the problems that are encountered daily in delivering the load would fill a library of books, but in closing with one story about the fickle English weather, I hope that all of us will appreciate the debt that is owed to this resilient band of people.

The story comes from Frank Strange, a man, now approaching retiring age, who has spent virtually all his working life — and quite a bit of his off-duty time as well — behind some form of steering wheel or another. He is a man who has seen much and has an obvious gift for words. We happened to be discussing the Lake District and his memory recalled this one journey across the Northern Hills.

'Still they talk about Shap, it was a devil in its time to be sure, but we could get enough aggravation on the A66, as it used to be. It's hard to believe how long it used to take us from Scotch Corner to Penrith or vice versa. So far as that goes though I have had some hairy runs over the same road in quite recent times and an incident of three or four years ago comes to mind. Not exactly Christmas, early February to be more precise. Seddon Atkinson 400 artic with a Rolls-Royce 220 engine and six-speed gearbox; 20 tons of 40 ft joists on a 40 ft semi-trailer, just about right.

'I'm an early morning man and usually start around 3 am but this time I reckoned we would go a bit earlier and turned out at 1.30 am, ringing Penrith police while eating my corn flakes. No, they said, there was no snow on the A66, but the M6 was running single lane from below Tebay. That's what I like to hear, since I prefer the former way anyway. We are into action at 2 am reaching Scotch Corner at 4.30 in cold, dry conditions again which I like. There is a slight delay there while someone tows a non-starter into life from out of the lay by, tearing a light cluster off in so doing, but its still dry even though I have a feeling in my bones that snow is coming. Quickly away again and we are hammering away up towards Greta Bridge. Funny though, only one Scotsman is seen going the other way and he has snow falling off his sheeted load.

'It's hard to believe but I had the A66 to myself for miles. The Rolls-Royce thunders down on to the Greta stretch of dual carriageway and away up the hill towards the chapel. Galley Bank comes into sight and it takes second gear before we clear it, then the snow starts to fall. Big flakes, half crown size and faster than the wipers can clear the screen. I batter it through Bowes and get the Roller to work on the climb up Spital Park with us still taking it on the nose, but she isn't slipping — not yet anyway. I notice headlights behind, it looks like a Bedford TK and he settles into my tracks. By this time we are up on to Stainmoor as we really start to work with the snow coming like it does round where I was brought up way back. I have good tyres and they are taking it nicely but its third gear work and I will have to be down into second soon. I'm just dropping down the box as we find a partly jack knifed artic and I still don't know how we found room to pass him, but we did and the TK followed.

'I know the road well and I am betting the Brough snowplough will be at work, but first we have to reach his patch and it is getting almost too bad to continue. But we are still under way and I don't give

No matter what the changes in cargo-carrying vehicles, we should never forget it is the driver who has to absorb the changes in technology as well as live with the fickle English weather. Bulk Liquid's Scammell artic tanker driver has paused for refreshment in one of Consett's many snow storms during 1962.

up easily. Suddenly the TK behind me disappears and I can guess what has happened but just cannot help. And then its over. The Brough ploughman is turning round and he flashes his headlights to tell me its clear forward. I thank him by lamplight and run down to Palliard Bridge then past the Punch Bowl down on to Brough. It's still lovely right to Coupland, but it isn't at Kirby Thore and some blokes are having a hard time working east towards Scotch Corner but I daren't stop. Finally Penrith comes into sight with the M6 almost clear from then on. Into Scotland there is no snow at all and after daybreak it's a lovely sunny day.

'The pay off to being an early starter is that I am an early finisher and we are soon comfy in the digs that I like to use on that run. Men are chatting as I try to watch television. They are curious as to which way I came up that morning so I tell them, without too much detail. What time did I come over the hills? Early enough. Did I see anyone else? Good question so we have to forget the telly as we talk about work again. The discussion considers that I was the last man to cross the A66 on that day as it is now completely closed with, they say, even the Brough snow plough blocked in at Stainmore. That figures but I hope the ploughman was safe. From all this I know we shall have to go the long way round, over the M62 to get home and sure enough when I reach Penrith there is a police road block on the entrance to the A66.

'Courtesy calls for me to spend the time of day as they direct me to use another route. As I turn to leave them — engine running and heater full blast — one officer tells me that it was a bad day on the hills yesterday and it still has not been cleared, but a steel lorry was seen about 6 am the previous day coming off the old road. He is considered to have been lucky or plain crackers.

'I feel it was the former, providing it was me that they were talking about. Crackers? Not quite. For remember while I knew it would snow I was too far committed to turn back and had I done so, which way could we have gone? The other roads even then were in a dicey state and the load had to get to Glasgow.'

IFF
INTERNATIONAL FERRY FREIGHT L